The Living Wisdom of
SOCRATES

The Living Wisdom of
SOCRATES

MARK FORSTATER

HODDER
MOBIUS

For Dorothy

'And I will comfort you as a mother comforts her children.'

For Jo

And the beautiful life we have together.

Copyright © 2004 by Mark Forstater

First published in Great Britain in 2004 by Hodder and Stoughton
A division of Hodder Headline

The right of Mark Forstater to be identified as the Author
of the Work has been asserted by him in accordance with the
Copyright, Designs and Patents Act 1988.

A Mobius Book

1 3 5 7 9 10 8 6 4 2

A CIP catalogue record for this title
is available from the British Library

ISBN 0340 73318 7

Typeset in Sabon by Palimpsest Book Production Limited,
Polmont, Stirlingshire

Printed and bound by Clays Ltd, St Ives plc

Hodder and Stoughton
A division of Hodder Headline
338 Euston Road
London NW1 3BH

CONTENTS:

Part Two: SOCRATES AND THE GENERAL

Part Three: THE VERDICT

ACKNOWLEDGEMENTS

I first began work on this book in 1999, and it was the first book that I (and not the influence of circumstance) chose to write, so I am very pleased that it has finally been published. When I consulted the I Ching to see what reception this book might have in the world, I received the hexagram Delight, and so decided that I should write the book in a state of delight, leaving any worldly anxieties away from the book's production. I wasn't completely successful in this, since the introduction was written during the protracted build-up to the attack on Iraq, a worrying time for us all. But thinking of the I Ching's prophecy I managed to keep myself in a reasonably positive state of mind for much of the time. Whether the book finds a delightful response in the world is not up to me or my publishers, but will be revealed in good time.

Besides the I Ching, I would like to thank my publishers, Ryan Harbage of Plume and Rowena Webb of Hodder Mobius, for helping this book find its way into print, and to my agent Liv Blumer for her continual encouragement.

I am grateful to Emma Heyworth-Dunn of Hodder Mobius for her insightful comments and editing suggestions.

I would also like to thank Rupert Lancaster of Hodder Audio, who has been very accommodating to all my audio ideas, and David Roper of Heavy Entertainment who has helped me record and edit them.

Since I am not a classical scholar I owe a huge debt to the many writers and academics whose work I have used (and I hope not abused) in coming to my own understanding of Socrates and his times. The list comprises among others:

Gregory Vlastos, A.E. Taylor, John Burnet, Hugh Tredennick, Robin Waterfield, Harold Tarrant, Robert S. Brumbaugh, Pierre Hadot, Michael Lerner, E.F. Schumacher, Jeremy Hayward, Morris Berman, Martin Buber, Henryk Skolimowski, Fritjof Capra, H.D.F. Kitto, Julia Annas, Anthony Gottlieb, Paul Davies, Joan Erikson, Jiddu Krishnamurti, Trevor J. Saunders, Danah Zohar, Thomas Berry, E.R. Dodds, Paul Weinzweig, Thomas A. Szlezák, Maurice Bowra, Alexander Nehamas, Terence Irwin, W.K.C. Guthrie, Giovanni Reale, Richard D. McKirahan, Phillip Vellacott, William Jordan, Josiah Ober, J.P. Mahaffy, Rex Warner, I.F. Stone, A.N. Whitehead, Bruno Snell, John Ferguson and many others.

Thanks to the British Museum for permission to use the photograph of Socrates.

Thanks to Mick Kidd and Chris Garratt for permission to use the Biff comic strip.

I would also like to thank Jeremy, Liane, Sian, Peter, Michaela, Maya, Sarah and my wife Jo for looking at the manuscript, and Jo for her patience in living with this sometimes distracted writer.

Modern civilisation can survive only if it begins again to educate the heart, which is the source of wisdom, for modern human beings are now far too clever to be able to survive without wisdom.
E. F. SCHUMACHER

INTRODUCTION

THE LOST TEACHINGS
OF SOCRATES

All the other sciences are more necessary and useful than philosophy, but none is superior to it.   ARISTOTLE

I first read about Socrates when I was a first year student at Temple University in Philadelphia, where I grew up. The text I studied, Plato's *Apology*, is probably the most widely read of all philosophical works, since it is a beautifully written and moving account of one man's justification for the philosophical life. The *Apology* is Plato's account of Socrates' trial, when the seventy-year-old philosopher was brought to court on charges of impiety and corrupting the young, was found guilty by his fellow Athenians and sentenced to death. His crime was his insistence on telling the truth, with no concern about the consequences. He had a mission, as he saw it, given to him by the god Apollo, to try to convince his fellow citizens to live lives that were ethically good, just and beautiful, and since this mission involved exposing their muddled and deluded thinking, there was no way that he could keep shtum, even for self-protection. Only death could silence him and end his mission.

I remember being struck by Socrates' heroic courage, his unwillingness to beg the court for mercy, and his quiet insistence that his mission was the most important public activity that he could offer his beloved Athens. I also liked his sense of humour. When he was found guilty, and was asked to name his punishment, he asked for free meals for the rest of his life at the Pyrtaneum, the banqueting hall where former Olympic champions dined at public expense. One can imagine how this went down with the jurors! Someone who could take this jokey attitude at a trial for his life showed either incredible stupidity or impressive strength of character. What I didn't understand at the time was how it is possible for someone to deliberately cultivate this kind of excellent character. I had assumed that Socrates' strength was inborn, part of the genetic make-up that he inherited from his parents. But I now know that his power, the enormous strength of his personality, was self-created and self-developed through his philosophy, through the way he lived his life, and the way he used his body, mind and soul.

When I returned, after nearly forty years, to look again at the figure of Socrates, I did so with a different perspective of my own. Over the past thirty years, I have been reading and studying the texts of many Eastern religions and philosophies – Taoism, Buddhism, Hinduism – and their approach to life is, on the surface, completely different from traditional Western philosophy. Yet Socrates, seen from an Eastern perspective, appears similar to a Taoist sage or a Hindu yogi. Like them, he is interested in wisdom and its practical use in the world. He has their same interest in cultivating his body as well as his mind, and he sees the world in a holistic and integrated way.

Socrates discovered the importance of soulful living as the basis for the good life. For him, happiness could only be achieved by someone who was acutely concerned with the state of his or her soul, and in keeping it healthy. Socrates embodied this philosophy in his own life, in that he was a completely integrated and holistic person. He brought together in his own person physical training for his body as well as a belief in the power of his rational mind, and at the same time did not ignore the non-rational or intuitive side of his self.

4

All these aspects of himself: the feelings, emotions, thoughts, physical impulses and intuitive insights together formed the self or person as he saw it, and the aim of the philosophical life was to make certain that this integrated holistic self maintained a healthy equilibrium in life. This meant that inner and outer experience was in balance, with the self fully integrated into family life, the larger community, and society as a whole, as well as being in harmony with the natural world.

I find it ironic that Plato, his most loyal student, actually distorted Socrates' main ideas about the soul, and in doing so encouraged the mind-body split that has so badly damaged our Western way of life. This split has given us the sense of being lonely ghosts in a clockwork universe, strangers in a strange land, whose alienation expresses itself through a proliferating and life-denying technology. This situation arose because Plato, influenced by Pythagorean ideas, came to believe that the soul was utterly different to the body, with qualities of a different order and magnitude. This led him to believe that the soul was immortal and merely imprisoned in a temporary, dense and lifeless body, and that it was the job of each person to free the soul from the body as much as possible in his or her lifetime. At death, the soul could rise free and join the absolute deathless world, while the body would merely decay. This divergence, from an integrated, unified view of the person held by Socrates, to the separated, dualistic view held by Plato, has helped to create the body-denying views of Christianity and the mechanistic conceptions of Descartes. Socrates' original ideas, what are in effect his 'lost' teachings, were healthy and life-enhancing, and led to a sense that the world was a natural and sustaining home for human beings. He intuitively understood the ecological perspective that we are living organisms enmeshed in a great co-operative web of creation, which supports us even as we support it. Today we are on a quest to discover how to live that same unified holistic way of life. In this quest of ours, Socrates, as a trailblazer, can show us the way.

THE SEARCH FOR
NEW VALUES

One purpose of philosophy is to demythologise power. Philosophy began in the Greek world in the sixth century BCE by seeking a total vision of life. The very first philosophers, the Pre-Socratics, asked basic questions about what the world was made of and how it worked. In answering these questions, they invented our idea of Nature and dismantled the old Olympian gods; the gods ceased to have power and became transformed into myth. The early philosophers' insights led to the Age of Science, and we are living at the tail end of that age.

Now the task of philosophy is once more to ask basic questions about our lives and the universe, and in doing so we may well have to transform old and outworn truths into a new set of myths, the myth of science. Today, philosophy's task is to demythologise our now dominant myths of science, technology, progress and unlimited economic growth. These myths of power are our contemporary idols, and it is a momentous and frightening thing to destroy your idols. But our degraded environment, continuous wars, worldwide poverty and disease show us the outcome of our current 'philosophy', which raises material powers to an unassailable height, while denigrating our spirit and denying us simple dignity and respect. We have to establish a new image of humanity and nature, an image that is sustainable for the future, and in doing so we will come to understand that the truths of science that we have based our lives on for the last three hundred years are no longer truths but myths, and need to be abandoned.

The old values that Western society relies on have been discredited and are largely empty of meaning. If we continue to model our lives on them we will find ourselves increasingly lost and in despair. The old values no longer work because they represent an old paradigm, a way of understanding the world that no longer fits reality. The picture of reality that we have been taught by parents and teachers does not correspond to the new vision of reality that twentieth-century science has discovered. But this new vision has not yet filtered down to a popular level and shaped the way we see the world, so we are conditioned by our upbringing to live according to an old cosmology, one that no longer corresponds to reality. The concepts held in our mind no longer mirror the structure of the world, and if we continue to live our lives out of sync with reality, then our values no longer fit with the way things really are, and we drift further into incoherence and confusion. We now have a need to discover, or rediscover, values that do work, that fit with the new reality. This is traditionally the work of philosophy, to understand the whole, the totality of things, and to search for the meaning of the whole.

Just as the Pre-socratics had done, we need to discover a truly integrated and holistic science and to dismiss the old science as myth. We are living at the turning point of two distinct paradigms approaching collision, the old one dying but still powerful, and the new one growing but not yet strong. It is our responsibility, and one that philosophy can provide the tools for, to understand intellectually this clash of old and new, and to mindfully live inside the new and rising one.

This is where Socrates and philosophy have a role to play. Socrates' greatest gift to us was to understand that the essence of being human is our human spirit, and his teachings are

7

concerned with how to nurture the entire person in order to live a good, positive and healthy life. Today we are not only in danger of losing our souls, but we are ignorant of exactly what the soul is and why it is essential to our lives. It is of the utmost importance that we rediscover not just what it is, but how we can live our lives to sustain and develop the spiritual and soulful side of life. If we can learn how to care properly for our spiritual selves, we gain access to our deepest feelings of compassion and tenderness, and even if these feelings are first directed only to ourselves, we will soon be able, quite naturally, to extend these finest of human feelings to other people, to all living creatures, and to the world itself. If we fail to recover our souls, we may well find that the earth no longer wants to sustain us as a living species, and we could follow the dinosaurs into oblivion.

A NEW PORTRAIT OF SOCRATES

Socrates was the first philosopher who was concerned with human values, who wanted to discover the essence of what it meant to be human. His aim was to illuminate the principles by which one could live a life that was fulfilling, that led to happiness and not to suffering or pain. In doing so he was the first person to reveal that what made us human was our souls, and the way we treat our souls makes the difference between suffering and happiness. He was on a similar path to the Buddha, a near contemporary, who also wanted to find a method to eliminate pain and suffering. Socrates lived his life not only in intellectual pursuit of these principles, but also embodied them in the way he related to himself and to others. He not only talked the talk, but he walked the walk, because ideas and concepts easily turn into arid intellectualism unless these ideas are shaken out and taken into daily life, used in homes, schools, businesses and shopping malls, to prove their effectiveness in ordinary human activity.

Socrates never wrote a word of philosophy, left us no texts to study, and never created a systematic philosophical structure through which to view all of life. So why is he still the most famous philosopher who ever lived? When he died, many of his followers wrote about him, partly to keep his memory alive, and partly to explain, justify and defend his life. Two of these students were Plato, who followed his master's example and became a philosopher himself, and Xenophon, a commander and military man who became an historian. Both Plato and Xenophon wrote dialogues in which Socrates is shown doing what he enjoyed most, roaming the city and questioning others about life's issues and problems. It is largely from their writings that we know anything at all about the mature Socrates, but there is a great disparity between the man presented by Plato and the one described by Xenophon.

Plato's Socrates is shown as an incisive, ironic and probing thinker, constantly engaged with the world of ideas, while Xenophon's Socrates is more often concerned with the practical and everyday problems of his friends and associates. If Plato's Socrates is a portrait of the philosopher as a seeker after wisdom, then Xenophon's portrayal is more of a cracker-barrel philosopher, a dispenser of conventional wisdom and grandfatherly good advice. Since most academics have an intellectual bias that assumes Plato's version must be closer to the truth of the historical Socrates, Xenophon's *Memorabilia*, after achieving great popularity in Roman and Victorian times, has become relegated to the remainder shelf.

But Nietzsche, a fine analyst of the Greeks and their thought, wrote:

> *If all goes well, the time will come when, to develop oneself morally-rationally, one will take up the* Memorabilia *of Socrates rather than the Bible . . .*

That is some prediction, and perhaps the time is now right to look at Xenophon's work again, to place it alongside Plato's in order to find a different perspective on the philosopher. For too long we have relied on Plato alone for our picture of Socrates, and there is value to be had in discovering a more down-to-earth and mundane Socrates, one whom we can easily relate to, through the lens of Xenophon. This will give us a more balanced view of the philosopher, and enable us to understand how he used his wisdom in ordinary human relationships and activities.

In Part One of this book, The Man Who Talked Himself To Death, I introduce Socrates, his life, the times he lived in and his teachings. I try to explain why his ethical teaching is more important now than ever before, and how Socratic philosophy can give us the means to make sense of a world that often seems brutal and meaningless. Philosophy has become of interest again because individually and collectively we are searching for a new set of values that we can live by. This is the same quest Nietzsche had when he postulated a 'revaluation of all values'.

In Part Two of this book, entitled Socrates And The General I include my version of a selection of dialogues and conversations of Xenophon. I have used as my starting point J.S. Watson's literal translation of the *Memorabilia* from 1871 which I have rewritten in contemporary English. I have made my selection and chosen the order so as to give a narrative structure to the relationship between the old philosopher and the young Xenophon, which stretches from their initial meeting to Xenophon's departure from Athens. To complete Socrates' story after this date, I have included in Part Three, entitled The Verdict, two early dialogues of Plato's dealing with Socrates' trial (the *Apology*), his time in prison (the *Crito*) and added the very brief description of his death as portrayed in the *Phaedo*. Here I have used as my basis the translations of Benjamin Jowett and again rewritten them in a more contemporary style.

Most collections of Socratic dialogues begin with the death of Socrates. I decided not to follow this order, but to begin my selection with the living philosopher and his relationship to the young Xenophon before ending with the trial and death, as detailed by Plato, who witnessed the event. I hope this order, combining the two writers, will give us a new portrait of Socrates: his life, activities, thoughts and death.

Socrates thought that the best way he could spend his time on Earth was to ask questions about the fundamental principles of human life, and chief among these is the question of justice. We too must ask these questions and find answers if we want to create an equitable and peaceful world, one that allows us individually and collectively to find peace and satisfaction. The tools for answering these questions can be found in philosophy's rich (and, until recently, forgotten) cupboard. For philosophy to become once again a contemporary way of life we must deliberately and consciously live by certain values that give it meaning, and it is only by discovering and holding to these authentic values that the life we want – a full, rich life – can be lived.

What is it that we consider our greatest value? Freedom – and especially the freedom of the mind. Balzac said, 'The world belongs to me because I understand it', and the philosophical quest is one for understanding both ourselves and the world we inhabit. Socrates said that at heart his teaching was very simple. It was merely to follow, with the utmost truth and sincerity, the saying carved on the Temple of Delphi – Know Yourself. This inner knowledge, which leads to the knowledge of the soul, is the most important knowledge we can learn, because it can transform our lives. For it is only by intimately knowing our deepest heart's core that we are able to understand other people, and this understanding enables us to discover the full integration of self and other, body and soul, individual and society. Indeed, our future on this planet may depend on a worldwide transformation of this kind.

Part One

THE MAN WHO TALKED HIMSELF TO DEATH

THE UGLIEST MAN
IN ATHENS

*We generally regard the utterances of a sage as being
at odds with the notions held by ordinary people*   HAKUIN

There is a story about Socrates that tells us a great deal
about his personal struggle to develop the character he
presented to the world. It's reported that Zopyrus, a face-
reader, was shown a portrait of Socrates, and was asked to
read his character. Zopyrus, unaware that it was a portrait
of the philosopher, said of the broad-faced, thick-lipped,
heavy-lidded, snub-nosed face that it was a classic portrait of
a sensualist, a man driven by ferocious lusts and appetites,
the holder of a fierce temper and violent emotions, with
strong Dionysian impulses to greedily experience the life of
the senses. Everyone found this amusing, because they knew
Socrates as the most disciplined and self-controlled of people,
a traveller of the middle way, who always prided himself on
mastering his impulses and senses.

But when Socrates was told the story, he surprised everyone
by agreeing completely with the face-reader; he recognised
himself as that sensualist, and acknowledged that his life had
been spent learning how to control and creatively transform
his sensuality into more important activities and not allow
himself to fall into dissipation.

Joan Erikson, in her book *Legacies*, makes an interesting

point about Socrates' looks. He was remarkably ugly in a society that worshipped beauty even more than we do. How did he cope, growing up as an ugly duckling in a society that valued physical perfection and found pleasure in looking at statues and paintings of the most graceful bodies and faces? In Socrates' time the concept of beauty had acquired importance as an expression of inner beauty, implying that someone of high spiritual and moral values would have an equally pleasing external appearance. The downside of this idea is that an unattractive face suggests inner ugliness, low morals and an evil character. She makes the point that, 'If, as a child, Socrates suffered from the shame of ugliness, it probably later became a goad for his intellectual and spiritual development.' Perhaps he developed his skill at argument and discussion as a virtue to offset his looks. This probably gave him a special quality and made him sought after, even though he was grotesque-looking.

The mature Socrates resembles the faces carved on statues of satyrs, and Plato plays with this resemblance in his *Symposium*, a wonderful account of a dinner and drinking party, where Alcibiades, the beautiful bisexual aristocrat – rich, powerful and glamorous – compares Socrates to those ugly figures of Silenus (the satyr) that are 'hollow inside, and when they are taken apart you see that they contain little figures of gods'. Often these gods were made of pure gold. Though the outer may appear grotesque and unattractive, inside, hidden away, there are heavenly treasures, which is always the way with sages.

Perhaps it was because Socrates' façade was so ugly that he became interested in developing his internal powers and cultivating an inner harmony. The Greek term for this perfect cultivation was *aretē*, which is often translated as virtue, although its meaning stretches far beyond the term virtue, which for us has mainly moral connotations. It's more meaningful for us to consider *aretē* as signifying excellence or success or the qualities that account for it. A person with *aretē* is the outstanding member of a group, someone with notable qualities of mind/body, someone perfectly adapted to succeed in a particular field. It implies a certain aptness or 'fitness' in the ecological sense.

In Socrates' case, this fitness can be seen in his inner qualities, which could not be seen by others because of his ugliness, but which could be felt by them as a kind of charisma. The influence of this charisma led them to rate him highly and gave Socrates a uniqueness, a reputation for his abilities. This was his *aretē*, and Socrates' concern was to discover how a person could develop this fitness or excellence, and, if a person had it, whether it was possible to teach it to someone else. Can *aretē*, success or excellence or fitness, or as the usual translations say, virtue, be defined and explained, and if so taught?

2

SOCRATES
THE MEDITATOR

There is a second story about Socrates, also from the *Symposium*, that is also emblematic about the man, and may help to explain how he developed those inner powers that gave him such strength of character. Alcibiades remembers a time when they were soldiers together at the campaign against Potidaea:

> A problem occurred to him early one day, and he stood still on the spot to consider it. When he couldn't solve it he didn't give up, but stood there contemplating. By the time it was midday other soldiers noticed him, and remarked with wonder that Socrates had been standing wrapped in thought since early morning. Finally, in the evening, after dinner, some of the soldiers brought their bedding outside – it was summertime – where they could rest in the cool and at the same time keep their eyes on Socrates to see if he would stand there all night as well. He remained standing until it was dawn and the sun rose. Then he made a prayer to the sun and walked away.

Not only does this story show the physical endurance that Socrates was famously capable of, but also his tenacity and mental concentration. This kind of contemplation, standing fixed in one spot, was not a unique occurrence. It seems that Socrates often had to separate himself to meditate. The *Symposium* begins with Socrates walking to the party with a friend, and then dropping behind in a fit of abstraction. He stands still in the portico of a neighbouring house, and contemplates alone until he is satisfied with the results of his meditation. When the other guests wonder what he is doing, they are told that he often stops and ruminates like this.

That Socrates used contemplation and meditation in his life is not surprising; it would illuminate a number of things about him. It may in fact be helpful, in order to gain a new perspective, to think of him as a yogi, someone whose main interest and activity is in gaining mastery of his mind, which is what yoga is intended to achieve, as explained in the Yoga Sutras:

> *Yoga means to control and still the swirling currents of thoughts in the mind. If you can control the thoughts that arise, and still them completely, you are able to observe the world clearly and directly without the distortions of the ego. The ability to discipline the chattering mind is what takes us to the state of yoga.*

Yogic contemplation and meditation are a means to an inner illumination, a revealing of the self. The yogi trains his mind to lose all attachments to objects of desire, and through this non-attachment completely frees himself from the desire for things worldly or spiritual. Socrates, as someone who was powerfully attracted to the world of the senses, could well have practised a form of yogic non-attachment: a separating or detaching of his powerful sensual energy from external objects of desire, whether attractive faces, bodies, money or objects. By separating his energy from his desires, he would have freed up that energy for other mental and spiritual pursuits.

There are two types of yogic meditation which Socrates may have used. The first is concentration and meditation on a single object like a flame, or an abstract idea like a colour. The second kind of meditation is when there is no object or idea to concentrate on, but only consciousness itself.

I can imagine Socrates using the first kind of concrete meditation to help him think through and clarify his ideas about a specific idea, problem or question. The second kind of abstract meditation, without an object to think about, could have helped develop the mental strength and stability that seems so characteristic of him. If he was as much of a sensualist as the face-reader claimed, then meditation could well have been the means he used to explore, divert, and transform those strong impulses and emotions from an obvious and direct physical expression to a more spiritualised dimension.

In order to control your impulses, you need to understand that they exist, that they are powerful, and that it is possible to exert control over them, and not become a passive victim of them. This kind of understanding can come from extended periods of meditation, when you are forced to confront who you really are and what it is that makes you tick. Meditation is a means of delving into the unconscious, and uniting the conscious mind with the knowledge and contents of the unconscious. Since Socrates believed in the rightness of the Delphic Apollo's dictum, Know Yourself, it's possible that it was through intense periods of meditation that Socrates developed his own inner knowledge, his inner illumination of who he was, what he believed in, and how he should live his life.

In meditation, you also learn to detach from the thoughts and feelings that constantly arise, so that the mind begins to quieten, and a certain state of calm serenity emerges, in which the true essence, the Self, is reflected. When you become aware of this true Self, you reach a state of intuitive understanding, a state in which you instantaneously have correct reactions and make accurate decisions. Socrates said at his trial that he had the gift of a certain divine sign, an inner silent voice, that at certain times signalled to him that something he wanted to do was not good for him, and so warned him not to act. He said that this sign never failed in being correct, so he came to rely on it, even offering its advice to others.

You have often heard me talk of the oracle that speaks to me, and is the sign or spirit or divinity that Meletus ridicules in the indictment. This sign has been with me ever since I was a child. It is a voice which comes to me and always forbids me to do or say something I am planning on, but it never encourages me.

I interpret this inner voice or oracle as Socrates' inner self making itself known to him as a form of intuitive understanding. It is clear that the sign does not emanate from his conscious reason and so must be part of his irrational mind. Was it in the profound silence of meditation that he became aware of this internal oracle, in the same way that the early Indian rishis, sages and yogis reported their inner discoveries in the Upanishads, the ancient Hindu religious texts:

The great teacher Prajapati said: 'The Self is pure, free from decay and death, free from hunger and thirst and free from sorrow. This is the Spirit in man. The only thing this Spirit desires is truth. This is the Spirit that we must seek and know: we must each find our own Self. When we have found our Self and gotten to know it, we have reached the ultimate, and there is nothing more to desire.

What this reliance on his intuition tells us is that Socrates, for all his insistence on a rational approach to life, was a person who balanced reason and intuition, so that he was able to approach life using all sides of his mind – rational and mystical. This kind of inner understanding comes from an intuitive and instinctive knowledge rather than from rational knowledge, which relies on the deliberations of our conscious mind and grasps things in a conceptual, intellectual, cerebral way. Inner, intuitive knowledge is more fundamental and holistic than rational knowledge since it emerges from the whole person, and comes as much from the body as from the mind. Combining conscious learning and unconscious knowledge, we instinctively feel that intuitive knowledge is a reflection of our total experience and so is closer to the truth of life. Thus, wisdom can be seen as a combination of life experience, intuitive understanding, and rational knowledge.

Intuitive understanding is not the knowledge of how a car or electricity works or what the square root of a number is (although we might like to know all of these things), but is the inner knowledge that we all possess, the simple certainty that tells us when we are hungry, thirsty, sleepy or that we have a headache or feel sick. This is a visceral, secure knowledge that we can trust because it tells us directly about the state of our mind, body and soul, and on this knowledge we are able to act. This subjective knowledge is more important and fundamental than the objective knowledge of how the world works, since inner knowing deals directly with our life energy, the force that maintains us in good health and continues our existence. Socrates' reliance on the saying Know Yourself reflects the understanding that we can only know other people and the external world accurately through having knowledge of our inner self.

3

THE STREET PHILOSOPHER

Socrates' solid sense of self enabled him to devise and cope with a very unusual lifestyle. He wore a single coarse woollen cloak in all seasons, and he walked barefoot through the Athenian streets, not bothered by excessive cold or intense heat. Towards the end of his life he was poor and lived simply and frugally with his wife and sons in a house he very likely inherited from his parents. He earned no money from teaching, since he refused to ask his followers or associates for payment, as other teachers did. In fact, he did not call himself a teacher since he insisted that he was ignorant himself and so had nothing to teach. He claimed that all he really knew was that he knew nothing, and this willingness to be the eternal student kept his mind unconditioned and open. Socrates was not ashamed of his poverty, and thought that simple living was a great benefit. The gods, he claimed, looked after those who made the smallest demands on them.

Socrates' lifestyle was intended to give him the maximum freedom to wander through Athens' exercise fields, market-places, shops and other public spaces where he could engage in a dialogue with his fellow citizens. If he had accepted money then he would be obliged to speak to paying customers, but since he was a free man he could stop and talk to anyone who was willing to talk to him. Socrates was a sort of intel-lectual street person, hanging around talking about whatever he found of interest. Since this activity was quite amusing and engaging – he often ended up getting kicked or beaten for exposing someone's threadbare 'philosophy' – he always attracted an audience, and this audience was often made up of the young sons of the land-owning aristocracy who had plenty of leisure time on their hands. This is how people like Xenophon and Plato became his followers, forming an audience of admirers for Socrates' demolition of traditional and commonplace sets of values.

But there was an important reason why Socrates took to the streets in this way. He explains in his defence speech why he was always engaged in this activity,

> . . . while I have life and strength I shall never cease from the practice of philosophy, advising and searching for the truth from everyone I meet. I shall go on saying, in my usual way, 'My friend, why do you, a citizen of the greatest and most famous city of the world for its wisdom, care so much about accumulating the greatest amount of money, glory and status, and so little of wisdom, truth and the improvement of your soul, which you never pay the slightest attention to? Aren't you ashamed of this?'
>
> If someone claims to care about his soul, I don't abandon him or let him go, but interrogate and examine and cross-examine him, and if I think he has no excellence (virtue/aretē), but only says that he has, I criticise him for neglecting what is of prime importance, and giving all his attention to trivialities.

He was always trying to convince them that *aretē* – success, excellence or fitness – was not shown or found by the possession of valuable objects, money or status, but that all these things would inevitably follow from the full possession of *aretē* of the soul, the development of inner beauty and harmony. Socrates taught that the most important thing in life was to care for one's soul, to keep it healthy, pure and whole by not doing evil. By doing the right thing, by pursuing the good, you would be able to fulfil all of your potential and develop every one of your innate qualities. For Socrates this is the true path to happiness.

And it was through discussion and not through lectures or books that he tried to convince them, since he said, according to Xenophon,

> . . . *whatever excellent principles we have learned by our civilisation, principles by which we know how to live, we learned only through the medium of speech; and that whatever valuable instruction any person acquires, he also acquires by means of speech. Don't those who teach best use speech the most; and those who know the most important truths, can discuss them with the greatest eloquence?*
>
> *Why else do I sit here in the market place every day talking to people? Isn't it through speech that I try to communicate some knowledge and wisdom to you?*

The reason Socrates never wrote down any philosophy is not that he was lazy but that he must have felt that it was impossible for books to convey the ideas and truths that interested him, or more precisely the method by which he and his fellow speakers discovered these truths. A book could not engage in conversation, since its words are fixed and cannot be altered. Words are only symbols for concepts, which will change over time, like the weather. In any case books could never reproduce the vibrant living philosophy that he practised.

In his years of pacing the streets discussing and clarifying important ideas, Socrates invented the dialectical method, the co-operative means of philosophical give-and-take, of idea countering idea, that later philosophers built on. For Socrates, what sets humanity apart from the animals is our ability to communicate through speech. Speech is the end result of a process of reasoning, of inner thought, and thought emerges from our consciousness as a kind of miracle. He saw human consciousness as a spark of the divinity that we share with the gods. It is through consciousness, thought, reasoning and speech that we have been able to create our civilisation and culture, and only through this soulful capacity will we have the possibility in the future to sustain and reinvent it. So when Socrates enters the agora, or marketplace, to talk to people about justice or piety he is really using the gift of the gods – speech – to do the highest possible work, that of being a physician to their souls.

4

EXERCISING THE MIND

To realise that our knowledge is ignorance is best.
To regard our ignorance as knowledge is a disease.

TAO TE CHING

Just as the body needs exercise, so too the mind, to keep it in a state of fitness, must be kept active and lively. An unexercised mind is a conditioned mind in which ideas and opinions, taken in without examination from outside sources like parents, teachers and the media, will laze around like mental couch potatoes. In Socrates' concept of the examined life the mind is exercised, and these ideas and opinions are roused, taken out for a daily workout to see if they are actually fit for the job they are intended to do. And the good thing is that to take part in this exercise there are no machines to buy or fitness centres to join. Not only that, but the exercise of the mind (especially in middle-aged and older people) can help to improve memory and increase brain connections.

Socrates' mind exercise, his method of question and answer, the dialectic or *elenchus*, requires only two people who will sincerely and honestly discuss an issue together, and by this co-operative intellectual effort discover a level of knowledge and wisdom that neither could reach on their own. The issues and opinions discussed are usually important concepts governing human life: justice, respect, happiness, self-control, courage and so on, and the exercises help to disperse confusion and ignorance and lead to greater knowledge and clarity of these concepts. By working in careful question-and-answer through the ideas you hold, you are able to rid yourself of mistaken opinions, replacing ignorance with knowledge. It is an educational project with the aim of changing one's life for the better by having a clearer view of one's own mind.

By exercising the mind like this there is an increasing confidence in its ability to think clearly and a growth of capacity to express those thoughts well. It's no different than when we start any new physical exercise or regime. At first our body is embarrassingly unfit and incoherent but with practice it improves, becomes more supple and coherent. Our mind has vast capacities that we rarely use, so that once we learn something new, and learn it really well, we gain confidence that we can extend that capacity to other sorts of knowledge. Truth is a network or system and if we can gain one piece of real knowledge there is no reason why we cannot extend our learning over a larger portion of it.

This rational discussion of points of view, a debate over ideas, doesn't always lead to any obvious conclusion, but often ends in what the Platonic dialogues call *aporia*, a kind of dead end of dialogue, where the discussion fizzles out in confusion and disarray. In contrast, Xenophon's dialogues always come to a neat conclusion, and reading some older scholars you get the feeling that they are disappointed that Plato's dialogues don't always round the discussion off nicely with Socrates explaining in a few succinct words what justice is. But Socrates was a complex and subtle thinker, who knew that tying a neat bow around concepts like justice was not a simple matter. Were Socrates' discussions more like Xenophon's versions than Plato's? We have no way of knowing.

Although the results are often negative, Plato never shows Socrates drawing sceptical or negative conclusions about the possibility of arriving at the truth. Instead, each new discussion represents a fresh start which will have unanticipated twists and turns depending on the unique minds, ideas and opinions of the people engaged in the discussion, and will arrive at different end-points from all previous discussions. Socrates' method is a living process that is creative and open-ended, and gives each participant the chance to explore, at their own speed, the theories and concepts they hold. His willingness to question makes him a potentialist and not a determinist. He is willing to suspend judgement and not come to a quick or even definitive answer, living with irresolution, an advanced kind of flexibility.

This process is a disinterested quest for truth, but knowledge is not the desired end in itself. The end that is sought is a development and improvement of human character, a positive transformation of the soul brought about by the method of rational thinking and argument. I believe that for Socrates the soul is identical with character, and the development of character is the ultimate aim both of his method and of life's many lessons.

The Pre-Socratic philosopher Heraclitus wrote, 'Man's character is his guardian spirit, or fate', and the German writer Novalis rewrote this as a famous aphorism: 'Character is destiny.' Both writers mean that it is our character, and not accident or chance, that determines the journey of our life, its events and outcome. Life is a series of largely unplanned and accidental events, but it is the way we react to them that determines our destiny, our fate. And because these two – life's events and our character – are completely interrelated, the combination of the events and our responses to them further develop our character. We can then say in reverse that 'fate or destiny develops character'.

But how does Socrates' method develop character? In Plato's dialogues we see that through Socrates' questions, the speakers become aware of contradictions and inconsistencies in their thoughts. This reveals that their philosophy of life (or what they might call their 'attitude' to life, if they are unaware they have a philosophy), is in serious error and they do not comprehend the world as it really is. They are faced with the fact that they are living in illusion and ignorance. If they are closed-minded and dogmatic this leads to frustration and anger (with Socrates, for showing them up), but if they have a sense of honesty and humility, are open to new ideas and have a willingness to stand corrected, then they can use these errors as a means to better organise all the fragmentary ideas in their mind. In other words, they can alter their ideas and thoughts and so change their underlying philosophy or attitude, and find a closer fit between their mind and the world.

Since the discussions are always intensely focused on important concepts and issues, there is a growing awareness of the essential principles behind the ideas, leading to a delineation or defining of the ultimate ends of human life. By partaking of this process of definition there is a progress in mental ability and a growth of spiritual knowledge, which leads to the excellence of the soul. As the mind becomes more open and aware of objective truth, so the soul is able to inhabit that truth, to live it, and this leads to spiritual progress. Perhaps, in Socrates' case, we can see that every advance of spiritual knowledge and capacity increased the strength and endurance of his will and helped to forge his powerful character. Is this why Socrates claimed that knowledge is *aretē* – excellence or virtue or good – and that someone who knows what is right can never do wrong? To have knowledge in this intimate way is to live it quite spontaneously, and if we live it we can never willingly go against it. But if we only know *aretē* as a slogan, a precept or an intellectual conceit, then we do not really live it, our soul does not partake of it, and so it is easy to go wrong.

Socrates also equated knowledge and *aretē* with personal happiness, claiming that to really know excellence, by living it day by day, *is* happiness. This interwoven trio of knowledge/excellence/happiness is very similar to the yogic trinity of sat/chit/ananda that equates to being/consciousness/bliss.

To have a consciousness or knowledge of our own inner being (our soul's excellence) is to be in a state of bliss, joy or happiness. The popular image of philosophy may be of a deep, objective, intense, rational and difficult pursuit of ideas, but for Socrates the final aim of philosophy is to live a good and happy life, which he certainly felt he had achieved. This may not seem very ambitious, but then how many of us can manage it?

SOCRATES' LIFE AND TIMES: THE STONEMASON AND THE REBUILDING OF ATHENS

5

Socrates was born in 469 BCE to Sophroniscus, a stone-mason, and Phaenarete, whom Socrates describes as a midwife. Since the *polis*, or city-state, of Athens had no hospitals Phaenarete was probably not a professional midwife but a 'wise woman' who was skilful at helping mothers deliver their babies. Plato has Socrates describe his own activities in the dialogue *Thaetetus* as those of an intellectual midwife, helping people bring to birth new conceptions and ideas:

> ... the only difference is that my concern is not with the body but with the soul that is in labour. And the culmination of my art is the power to prove by every test whether the child of someone's thought is a phoney vision or is infused with life and truth.

But before he was able to devote himself fully to intellectual midwifery, he earned a living in his father's profession, carving stone statues and monuments, including, the ancient sources say, some of the figures on the Parthenon.

It was a good time to be a stonemason. The tiny Athenian city-state, after having helped the united Greeks defeat the much larger invading Persian army at Marathon in 490 BCE, and again ten years later, in 480, defeating them at Salamis, emerged from the Greek-Persian wars as an unlikely victor, having a positive, strong, vibrant democracy at home, and a string of Greek islands and cities in the Eastern Mediterranean as allies, providing Athens with the beginnings of a maritime empire.

The Athenian victory at Salamis was seen as a kind of miracle. Reluctantly following the advice of their leader Themistocles, the Athenians abandoned the city to the invading Persians and took refuge in their ships, carrying non-combatants and whatever property they could to the island of Salamis. From there they had to watch helplessly as the Persian army burned their houses and destroyed the holy temples on the Acropolis. But the Athenian act of collective desperation paid off when their agile navy outmanoeuvred the Persian fleet, scattering and destroying them.

The Greek triumph over the Persians, and in particular Athens' seminal role in this defeat, gave the Athenians a sense that their young democracy had come of age and proven its worth. It showed that a society where each citizen (meaning native-born men, but excluding women, slaves and foreigners) defended his own right to political power could triumph over one where power was restricted to a despotic king or a small group of aristocrats. It appeared that freedom and reason had finally defeated despotism and fear. The sense of euphoria and of exaltation, of unlimited horizons and of endless possibilities must have been overwhelming.

The rebuilding of the city, in particular the desire to recreate it as a beautiful and magnificent shrine to Athena and the gods who supported the citizens' heroic deeds, gave architects, carpenters, stonemasons, sculptors and painters an opportunity to show off their skill and be well paid for it. Socrates and his father would have been engaged on the continuous building of these famous temples and landmarks.

In 449 BCE a lasting peace was signed with the Persians, and the rebuilding of the temple of Athena Parthenos, now called the Parthenon, began. The statesman Pericles wanted the triumphant city and the political, ethical, religious and cultural values of its free and democratic people to be reflected in suitably grand architecture and art. It was this demonstration of civic pride that led to the creation of the series of buildings that circled the hilltop of the Acropolis. The Parthenon, which had been left unfinished in 460, was redesigned and rebuilt on an impressive scale.

Pericles worked closely with the artist and architect Phidias to create the first large-scale urban improvement scheme ever accomplished in the western world. Their aim was to develop Athens as the leading city of culture, the cultural capital of Greece; in doing so they created an unprecedented and unrivalled splendour that was to be the envy of the world. Society was seen as an harmonious equilibrium between the individual and the collective, between the public and the private, and the rebuilding of Athens attempted to express this perfect unity. The artists set themselves the task of also expressing the supreme beauty of both the visible and the invisible worlds: they wanted to portray in paint and marble the ideal of humanity. They succeeded so well that Athens became noted not only for her intellectual gifts of wisdom and virtue but also for her beauty.

In his famous Funeral Oration at the end of the first year of the Peloponnesian War, Pericles prophesied.

Mighty indeed are the marks and monuments of our Empire. Future ages will wonder at us, as the present age wonders at us now.

The city became an open-air museum, where the most striking works of architecture, sculpture and paintings were on permanent display, while the public theatres were home to music, lyric poetry and the great tragic dramas and comedies of

Aeschylus, Sophocles, Aristophanes and Euripides. The incredible victory over the Persians, the building of this magnificent city, and the growing power and influence of the Athenian empire gave the Athenian people the feeling that they were living through a golden age, one of endless possibility and potential.

This feeling was captured by Pindar in one of his victory odes, written for the winner of one of the many athletic competitions held in Greece:

He who wins, of a sudden, some noble prize
In the rich years of youth
Is raised high with hope; his manhood takes wings;
He has in his heart what is better than wealth.

Socrates was privileged to come of age in the midst of this extraordinary burst of Athenian energy and creativity, which he first witnessed as a young man and then added to with his own genius. This golden age of classical Athens, a unique period of some fifty years, developed partly because the institution of a direct and real democracy allowed the freeing of the collective spirit of the Athenians. It was a tremendous time to be alive. But Pindar went on to warn:

But brief is the season of man's delight.
Soon it falls to the ground; some dire decision uproots it.
– Thing of a day! Such is man; a shadow in a dream.

Yet when god-given splendour visits him
A bright radiance plays over him, and how sweet is life!

Brief also was the season of Athens' delight. Almost as if the city-state was the leading character in one of its own primal tragedies, the increasing pride, over-confidence and arrogance of Athens brought it falling to the ground when its citizens too made a 'dire decision' in wartime. Failing to understand the limitations of power they voted for a war campaign that lost them their sovereignty and for a time destroyed their democratic traditions. In the midst of despair and loss they turned on the dissident Socrates, blaming him for their collective errors. But that is a story for later.

6

THE NATURAL PHILOSOPHER

We know very little of Socrates' early life, but at some point he gave up the artisan life and became a student of the first Athenian philosopher Archelaus. It may be that his oldest friend Crito, a rich landowner, decided his friend's talents were wasted on stone, and gave him financial assistance. Socrates may also have made enough profit from financing ships' merchants to have retired temporarily from daily work. At this time he was a single man, with no family or commitments.

His teacher Archelaus was a student of the famous philosopher Anaxagoras, who spent thirty years in Athens before having to flee the city after being charged with atheism. Scholars include Archelaus and Anaxagoras as two of the 'Pre-Socratics', the philosophers who came before Socrates. The reason there is this fine line drawn between Socrates and the others is that Socrates is considered the first philosopher who became interested in ethical questions and human values, whereas those preceding him were mainly interested in cosmological and natural questions.

Socrates, as a student of Archelaus, seems to have started his career as a natural scientist interested in medical and psychological issues, but moved away from this study in late middle age. The playwright Aristophanes captures this early phase of Socrates' career in his comedy *Clouds*, written in 423 BCE where he shows the forty-six-year-old philosopher as the otherworldly head of a philosophical think tank-cum-commune, the 'high priest of subtle bilge', who denies that the gods cause rain, thunder and lightning (the traditional view), and instead claims that these phenomena are caused by the natural actions of the air and clouds, the new gods. In his play the political and religious conservative Aristophanes burlesques the activities and claims of the natural philosophers and uses Socrates as their figurehead.

There seems little doubt that Socrates started his philosophical career immersed in natural questions, but then underwent a conversion in late middle age. Plato has Socrates describe part of this conversion in the dialogue *Phaedo*:

> When I was young, I had a tremendous desire to know that part of philosophy called Natural Science; this seemed to me to have high aims, since it is the science which has to do with the causes of things, and that teaches why a thing exists, and why it is created and destroyed; and I was always agitating myself with such questions as these: is the growth of animals the result of some decay which the hot and cold principle contracts, as some have said? Is blood the element with which we think, or is it the air, or fire? Or perhaps nothing of this sort – but the brain may be the originating power of the perceptions of hearing and sight and smell, and memory and opinion may come from them, and science may be based on memory and opinion when no longer in motion, but at rest.

These kinds of questions relate to the interests and ideas raised by the natural philosophers, the Pre-Socratics. It's important to explore this first phase of Greek philosophy in more detail, because it will help us to understand the kinds of problems that Socrates wrestled with in his younger days, and these thinkers form the intellectual background to his later activities and philosophy.

Philosophy begins with the Pre-Socratic Greeks, who were its creators, and who gave to our civilisation something it did not possess before. From the moment of its birth, philosophy represented a new form of revolutionary intellectual and spiritual expression that changed the course of civilisation.

The early philosophers sought answers about the universe that would satisfy their reason, and this led them to look for a vantage point from which they could view all of existence, a point where the world would reveal all of her secrets. They began by making speculative hypotheses about natural phenomena, trying to discover 'Nature' as an entity separate from the gods.

This was the turning point in the Western intellectual tradition, when creative thought – insight – made a first attempt to discover what the world was made of. The Greek approach was very different to that of any earlier societies, which believed that God or the gods made the world, a belief which had to be unthinkingly accepted, and never questioned. But the Pre-Socratics believed that the causes of things, and how they acted, could be known by a questioning mind, and so they transferred the problems of nature and human nature from the realms of religious tradition and poetic intuition to that of the intellect.

And so philosophy began. The Pre-Socratics assumed that the universe is an intelligible whole. They presumed that a single order, a cosmos, would be found beyond the chaos of their sense perceptions and that by using their rational minds they could comprehend that order. A cosmos means an ordered universe and if they could show that the world was rationally ordered into a single world of being, they thought it would be one composed of goodness and beauty, and not one of moral or aesthetic neutrality. They began the search for the one principle or fundamental substance that was the common property and the material cause of everything, searching for the reality that lay beyond appearances.

The first of the Pre-Socratics was Thales of Miletus, an engineer and statesman, who invented the ideas of matter, of physics, of science and of philosophy. He held that 'Water is the material cause of all things'. He thought that the differences in things could be accounted for by the transformations of liquid, since water can flow, be turned into vapour when hot, and become a solid when cold; it also springs naturally from the earth, and is a primary condition for life. Although this idea sounds simple to us, we need to remind ourselves how revolutionary it was at that time, when most people believed the gods caused everything.

But Thales, although he did not believe in the official religion, was not an atheist. Professor John Burnet, in his book *Greek Philosophy*, says that, 'Greek philosophy is based on the faith that reality is divine . . . It was in truth an effort to satisfy what we call the religious instinct.' Philosophy and religion are closely tied together, and whenever one appears the other must follow. Thales wrote, 'The gods are in all things', meaning that all of nature is alive with a divine presence and is not dead matter. Thales sensed that there is an immanent divinity, a spirit, alive in the world, expressing itself through all of life.

Thales was followed by Anaximander, a mapmaker, who said that the primary substance could not be one of the elements like water, but had to be something more ineffable and subtle, something infinite, eternal, ageless and uniform that encompassed the world and had no definite specific characteristics of its own. He called it the boundless, and said, 'All things arise out of the boundless . . . and they make reparations and pay penalties to one another for the injustices they commit, according to the measure of time.' This idea of the see-saw of reparations and penalties relates to the language of courts of law; Anaximander was the first thinker to apply the idea of law to the physical world of nature.

Nature, unlike the Olympian gods, was not anarchic and capricious, but followed a certain order and balance in its actions, a pendulum effect similar to the cyclical Chinese idea of yin and yang. Anaximander saw that Nature's laws swing from one extreme to the other, one way leading to excess and then swinging back into a balance and harmony. This natural 'justice' in their concept of nature gave the Pre-Socratics a key to the right ordering of human life. They saw that nature was inherently divine and that it worked through a sense of justice, both cosmic justice and human justice.

One of the most enigmatic and insightful of the Pre-Socratics is Heraclitus of Ephesus, who expressed himself in terse, oracular statements that influenced most of the later Greek thinkers, and whose ancient speculations have been confirmed by contemporary science. Heraclitus thought that the world is composed of fire, in its many transformations of shape and form. Since current thinking is that the universe did start its existence with an enormous explosion, that our world began as a great ball of fire before it cooled, and that the sun, our source of life, is in essence a ball of fire, then Heraclitus does not seem so far off in claiming fire as some kind of first principle.

Heraclitus also said, 'You can't step into the same river twice,' since the water you stepped into the first time will have gone far away by the time you step in again. His belief was that everything is always moving, is always changing, and thus in a constant state of becoming rather than a state of static being. We are all in transition, are never static or at rest, but are always in a state of process or transformation. Our contemporary beliefs in an expanding universe and constant evolutionary change tie in well with Heraclitus's speculations. He understood that the universe is in constant flux, and the stability that we see in nature is only temporary, an illusion of time.

There were a number of other Pre-Socratic philosophers, each of them following a different line of thought, and as each theory was critically appraised in its turn there was a continuous inquiry into the nature of reality. This led to a progressive and cumulative increase of knowledge. Anaximenes thought that the essential element was air; Parmenides of Elea brought a purely logical element into play, and he argued and proved (to himself) that all change was an illusion, and that there was only One being, changeless and eternal. Empedocles, from Sicily, said that there were four basic elements: fire, air, earth and water, and they were mixed together by two primary actions, love and strife, which is what creates change in the world. His contemporary was Anaxagoras, and with him we come full circle to Socrates and his time.

7

MINDFUL ANAXAGORAS

Anaxagoras was a young scientist and philosopher who claimed that the heavenly bodies were stones, held aloft by their rapid spinning motion. People who heard this notion found it ludicrous, and had we been alive at the time we would probably have laughed at him as well. But one day in 467 BCE a tremendous meteorite fell to the earth at Aegospotami. This event gave credence to Anaxagoras's theory and is perhaps the reason why he was invited by Pericles to join his circle of cultural and political advisers. He lived in Athens for thirty years, eventually being driven out on a charge of impiety, since he held that the Sun, a god, was just a hot stone. His trial is a clear foreshadowing of the later trial of Socrates.

Anaxagoras wanted to explain how Heraclitus's theory of the world's constant flux would have worked. He proposed that all change is caused by the mixture and separation of infinitely small and infinitely numerous 'seeds' that compose all things. These 'seeds' are in everything but can change in proportion, depending on the composition of the object. He believed that all matter was a continuum, a constantly changing and flowing process. The aspect that was most original in his thought was that he brought 'nous' – mind or intelligence – into the equation, and this is what interested Socrates in his theories, as Plato recounts again in the *Phaedo*:

Then I heard someone who had a book of Anaxagoras, out of which he read that mind was the disposer and cause of all, and I was quite delighted at the notion of this, which appeared admirable, and I said to myself: If mind is the disposer, mind will dispose all for the best, and put each particular in the best place; and I argued that if anyone desired to find out the cause of the generation or destruction or existence of anything, he must find out what state of being or suffering or doing was best for that thing, and therefore a man had only to consider the best for himself and others, and then he would also know the worse, for the same science comprised both. And I rejoiced to think that I had found in Anaxagoras a teacher of the causes of existence such as I desired, and I imagined that he would tell me first whether the earth is flat or round; and then he would further explain the cause and the necessity of this, and would teach me the nature of the best and show that this was best; and if he said that the earth was in the centre, he would explain that this position was the best, and I should be satisfied if this were shown to me, and not want any other sort of cause. And I thought that I would then go and ask him about the sun and moon and stars, and that he would explain to me their comparative swiftness, and their returnings and various states, and how their several affections, active and passive, were all for the best.

What hopes I had formed, and how grievously was I disappointed! As I proceeded, I found my philosopher altogether forsaking mind or any other principle of order, but having recourse to air, and ether, and water, and other eccentricities. I might compare him to a person who began by maintaining generally that mind is the cause of the actions of Socrates, but who, when he endeavored to explain the causes of my several actions in detail, went on to show that I sit here because my body is made up of bones and muscles; and the bones, as he would say, are hard and have ligaments which divide them, and the muscles are elastic, and they cover the bones, which have also a covering or environment of flesh and skin *which contains them; and as the bones are lifted at their joints by the contraction or relaxation of the muscles, I am able to bend my limbs, and this is why I am sitting here in a curved posture: that is what he would say, and he would have a similar explanation of my talking to you, which he would attribute to sound, and air, and hearing, and he would assign ten thousand other causes of the same sort, forgetting to mention the true cause . . . There is surely a strange confusion of causes and conditions in all this. It may be said, indeed, that without bones and muscles and the other parts of the body I cannot execute my purposes. But to say that I do as I do because of them, and that this is the way in which mind acts, and not from the choice of the best, is a very careless and idle mode of speaking.*

As Plato presents it, Socrates starts his philosophical life as a natural scientist, but eventually becomes disillusioned with the dizzying variety of ideas and speculations of the natural philosophers, and the lack of a synthesis or agreement among their claims. Each philosopher presents a different cause for existence and a different cosmology, and since they can't all be right, it is impossible to tell the correct ideas from the incorrect ones.

When Socrates hears about Anaxagoras's theory that mind or intelligence is the ordering principle of life, this seems to satisfy his own wish to find a non-material but conscious controller or regulator of existence. If mind or intelligence is the power in the universe, then mind should be able to order everything that happens in the best possible way, and Socrates wants to hear how Anaxagoras explains this. If mind or reason is the cause of existence then reason can be used to assess all the other theories to determine which ones make sense.

Professor A.E. Taylor, in his book *Socrates*, puts it like this:

Mind, said Anaxagoras, is the cause of all natural law and order, just as mind is the cause of all orderliness and coherence of human action. To Socrates this suggested that the universe at large is the embodiment, like a properly conducted human life, of coherent rational plan. If Mind is the cause of the world's structure, the earth and everything else in the universe must have just the shape, position, place in the scheme, which it is best that each of them should have.

Socrates is clearly disappointed at Anaxagoras's unwillingness to allow mind or consciousness to do more than just be the originator or 'disposer' of matter. Anaxagoras declares that mind is essential as the originator of existence, but then finds no other role for it to play, which is a kind of incipient dualism. This disturbs Socrates, who was clearly looking for consciousness and reason to be given a more central role in the cosmos and in human life. Evidently, he had to work out his own cosmology and philosophy relating to consciousness, reason and human ethical concerns, and in doing so he was the first thinker to discover the human soul. This may be a strange idea to accept, since the soul does not seem to be something that can be discovered; somehow, we feel that it has always been with us. But Professor Giovanni Reale in his book, *From the Origins to Socrates* says:

The conception of the soul, although almost absent prior to Socrates, is widespread in the literature immediately following Socrates and is common to Isocrates, Xenophon and Plato. It is evident, therefore, that it must have had its origin either with Socrates or with some of his contemporaries; but we do not know of any contemporary of Socrates to whom we might attribute it, while we know from Plato and Xenophon that Socrates typically professed it in such a way that the attribution of the doctrine in question to Socrates becomes a practical necessity.

The scheme Socrates worked out involved a belief that the universe is providential, that there is a divine consciousness, spirit or mind existing in the cosmos which organises all of existence in an orderly, structured, harmonious and coherent way. If the universe is caused or created by a cosmic mind or logos, then our individual minds, which have been created by this cosmic mind, have an identity with it, and share in the qualities that make the universe what it is. The beauty of the natural world, the goodness of life, love, compassion, and all the excellent qualities that make up our world must flow from this abundant and coherent mind or spirit, and our individual consciousness partakes of all these qualities and functions. In Socrates' cosmology there is a direct and natural link between the conscious human world – the human spirit – and the conscious *logos* – the spirit of the universe. Micro and macro, life below and life above, share an identity which is composed of consciousness. For Socrates, the reality behind all appearances is this cosmic spirit, and this is the basis of truth, goodness and beauty.

Xenophon wrote a dialogue which I have called Aristodemus and The Gods (Part 2, Chapter 10) which details some of Socrates' conceptions of the relation of gods to humans:

SOCRATES: *'Nor did it satisfy the gods to take care of only the body, but what is most important of all, they implanted in us the soul, our most excellent part. For what other animal has a soul which understands, first of all, that the gods, who have arranged such a vast and noble order of things, exist? What other species of animal, besides man, offers worship to the gods? What other animal has a mind better equipped to guard against hunger or thirst, or cold or heat, or to relieve disease, or to acquire strength through exercise, to study to obtain knowledge; or is more capable of remembering whatever it has heard or seen or learned?*

'Do you suppose that the gods would have engendered

a belief in people that they are able to benefit or injure them, unless they were really able to do so, and that people, if they had been thus so perpetually deluded, would not have become sensible of this delusion? Don't you see that the oldest and wisest human communities, the oldest and wisest cities and nations, are the most respectful of the gods, and that the wisest age of man is the most observant of their worship?

'Consider also,' he continued, 'that your mind, existing with your body, directs your body as it pleases; and it becomes you therefore to believe that the intelligence pervading all things directs all things as may be agreeable to it, and not to think that while your eyes can extend its sight over many miles, that of the divine power is unable to see all things at once, or that while your mind can think of things here, as well as in Sicily or Egypt, that the mind of the deity is incapable of regarding everything in existence at the same time.'

This sharing of consciousness between the divine and the human leads Socrates to construct a simple philosophy built around the soul, which he identifies as the essence of being human. It is our soul that is the guide or 'orderer' of our individual life, and so a living philosophy must have as its aim the knowledge of this soul itself, as well as the wisdom of knowing how to nurture it.

From this follow the two Socratic precepts, 'KNOW YOURSELF', and 'TAKE CARE OF YOURSELF'. Knowing yourself is the theory of who you are in your deepest heart's core, while taking care of yourself is the practical means to spiritual progress. For Socrates, the aim of a human life is to liberate the full potential of the individual by perfecting the human soul, and through this liberation to achieve happiness. The soul loves the truth, and wants to join with it; therefore, the closer we can bring our individual souls into line with the cosmic universal spirit, the closer we are to living in truth.

This aim of protecting and liberating the human spirit by perfecting the soul leads to a set of values that can achieve this aim. These values relate to the nature of the human spirit and its affinity to the goodness and beauty of the cosmic spirit that is its model. To perfect the soul means to pursue goodness or beauty to achieve a certain *aretē* or excellence, and excellence is found in the famous 'virtues' of wisdom, courage, piety, self-mastery and justice. In fact all these virtues combine into one virtue, one *aretē*, whose maxim is 'do nothing that will harm your spirit'. Socrates believed that anything that harms the spirit takes us away from perfection, and therefore away from a closer affinity to the cosmic spirit, while the performance of the good takes us ever closer to the mark. Doing good, creating beauty, following justice perfect the soul and create the conditions for social harmony, while wrongdoing harms the soul and poisons our social relations.

Putting these values into action means having to answer at every one of life's moments that famous question of Socrates: 'what is the right way to live?' The Socratic way is to always question ourselves about our actions, and when we are uncertain whether what we are about to do will harm or help our spirit, we must rationally decide between the courses of action that we are considering. Reason is one of the tools in our consciousness kit which we can use to analyse whether what we are about to do is right or wrong, when right means the best way to nurture our spirit and wrong means to harm it. Justice, piety, wisdom are means to do the right thing, and to increase our spiritual qualities.

The spirit, both in its cosmic as well as its human manifestation, is the key to Socrates' philosophy. We can only understand the world through a total experience of life – our feelings, thoughts and sensations – and since the world as we know it is our experience or consciousness of it, the state of our consciousness dictates the world that we perceive. If our consciousness is the most important aspect of life, then our task is to keep that consciousness healthy and unsullied.

8

THE SOPHISTS AND SOCRATES' CONVERSION

It is not enough to know yourself. What is important is to be yourself.

NIETZSCHE

Human life moves in cycles from infancy to old age. There are phases, steps and crises in the life cycle, and at each stage we leave something behind and gain something new, but the strength of the process may lead in time to wisdom. Socrates' philosophical problems during the mid-life stage, when he was in his late forties or early fifties, indicates a possible mid-life crisis. Did he wonder now whether he had wasted his youth in foolish and idle speculation? In middle age what had he achieved? He may well have thought that he had accomplished nothing, knew nothing and was going to leave behind nothing to future generations. Having devoted so much of his working life to natural philosophy and derived so little satisfaction from it, his life, as reflected in that long passage in the *Phaedo*, appears to suffer from a lack of meaning. He may have become directionless, aimless, wondering what to do next. He was still a single man, rootless, directionless, but while he had spent years with his head lost in the stars, life around him in Athens had not remained at a standstill, but had markedly changed.

A new group of philosophers had arrived on the scene, calling themselves Sophists, or wise men. The Sophists had no interest in cosmological or scientific questions like the Pre-Socratics, and it was they who actually brought philosophy down from the skies to mingle with the ordinary world. They were concerned with human ideas and human problems, but their teaching was completely practical. They were concerned with immediate means, not ends, and their search was not for truth but for expediency and results, especially in the political arena.

Athens was a direct democracy, where any citizen could speak in the assembly or prosecute a law case. The ability to convince others of your ideas in the assembly, and success or failure in court depended almost entirely on individual speaking ability. The sons of rich landowners and aristocrats were brought up and educated with the confidence to speak well in public, but the sons of artisans, workers and traders had no such training. This opportunity for providing higher education was spotted by the Sophists who toured the various Greek cities like management gurus, giving demonstrations of their virtuosity and learning, and holding classes for private students. They taught mostly rhetoric and oratory, which meant techniques of persuasion. They believed these could be taught to anyone, whether artisan, trader or landowner, as long as they could pay good money for it.

The Sophists were not interested in searching for truth, but taught techniques to gain power and influence, to maintain self interest and to get one's own way. They were interested in imparting only worldly knowledge that could be put to use. The state of the soul was not their concern; they were interested only in becoming effective in the public eye.

Socrates was interested in the Sophists and met and talked with a number of them, meetings which are recreated in a number of Plato's dialogues. Socrates was intrigued by the most famous Sophist, Protagoras, and attended the Sophist Prodicus's one-drachma lecture (he claimed he couldn't afford the expensive ones). It is from Prodicus that Socrates got his interest in the exact nature of words and meanings, and the wish to search for definitions. Prodicus taught him that for each word there was only one specific meaning – for example *enjoyment* relates to activities of a mental nature, while *pleasure* is involved more directly with the body. Similarly, *wish* and *desire* are different, *wish* also being mental and *desire* involving the body and will and so on.

Protagoras had a saying, 'Man is the measure of all things', which was highly influential. While philosophers claimed to be seeking an absolute or unchanging truth, the perfect standard by which everything else could be judged, Protagoras, a postmodernist before his time, claimed that there was no absolute truth, only relative truths. He held that each person's subjective truth is equal to any other person's, and that there is no objective standard of truth to judge anything by.

In a democratic society this represents a kind of democratic version of the truth. If all citizens are equal then each person's version of reality is equally valid, and no distinctions of quality can be made between them. Because of this attitude, the Sophists became famous for being able to argue both sides of a question, which was one of the debating skills they taught. They didn't care if they had to argue for or against a question, as long as they won the debate.

This downgrading of truth, when carried to an extreme, has bitter consequences for society, as we are discovering today, when relativity of thought also rules. If there is no difference between one opinion and another, if there is complete equality between ideas and no distinction made between true and false, then anything goes, and there is no reason to hold back from thinking, saying or doing anything, no matter what the consequences. As long as a person can justify his actions to himself, no matter how harmful they may be to others, to society or the world itself, then that action is acceptable.

This distortion of individuality leads to a nihilistic attitude, which helps destroy community and the environment, and although it may give some individuals great wealth and power, it reduces the health and well-being of society as a whole. In Athens it led to a debased moral code that claimed that the strong man was superior to the crowd, could therefore follow his own selfish desires and despise and ignore the laws, which this code claimed had only been created by weak men to protect themselves against the strong. This philosophy of ruthless individuality led to a reckless hunger for individual power, fame and wealth, and was instrumental in the decline of Athenian democracy.

By the middle of the fifth century BCE the Sophist was the popular image of a philosopher, and it was inevitable that his fellow Athenians would bracket Socrates with them. I'm sure it was important for him to distance himself from the Sophists and to maintain his own image and independence. I believe it is from this need that many of his famous paradoxes arise. For example, I think Socrates refused to charge money for his talks because the Sophists only talked for payment, refused to admit that he knew anything because the Sophists claimed to know everything, and denied that he had anything to teach because the Sophists claimed the ability to teach everything.

Socrates' method of question and answer, the dialectical method, may even have developed as a response to the Sophists. The Sophists revelled in the role of wise men who knew everything and were able to answer all questions thrown at them. Socrates takes the exact opposite position, claiming to know nothing, and so claims he is unable to answer *any* questions put to him. Therefore, although he appears to be perverse in setting up a method in which he wants only to *ask* questions of others, and not to answer them himself, he is in fact setting himself up in his own niche. Socrates wants to be seen as an individual, a philosopher, someone who ceaselessly searches for human truth and human values, and has no need to act like the other wise men.

However, he did learn from the Sophists that there was a popular interest and need in ordinary people to discuss serious ideas and issues relating to daily life. Cosmology and natural science may have led him to an impasse, but there was another subject, of much more immediate importance, that he was interested in learning about and teaching, and this revolved around the question, 'how are we to live?' In focusing on this question Socrates invented the ethical quest and established his own unique method of Q and A.

But what was the catalyst that led him to begin this new life, to abandon scientific questions, and to take to the streets, discussing ideas with his fellow Athenians? What led to his ethical quest and his understanding of the human soul? He tells this story in the *Apology*, his defence speech:

> You must have known the late Chaerephon; he was one of my oldest friends, and was very impetuous in everything he did, and once he actually travelled to Delphi to boldly ask the oracle to tell him whether there was anyone wiser than Socrates, and the oracle answered that there was no one.
>
> When Chaerephon told me the oracle's answer, I said to myself, 'What can the god mean? What is the interpretation of this riddle? I know that I have no real wisdom, small or great, so what can he mean when he says that I am the wisest of men? He can't be lying, because he is a god; that would be against his nature.'

Reading the oracle's answer today, 2,400 years later, and knowing Socrates as the most famous philosopher in the Western tradition, it is impossible for us to comprehend how disconcerting and unlikely this answer must have seemed to him. His many years as a natural philosopher had come to nothing, he was very much a footloose student in relation to the celebrated Sophists, and although he was a well-known character in Athens, he had no reputation as a philosopher. Aristophanes' play must have done his public image no good at all. And yet, in the midst of all this negativity and disappointment, with all the brilliant minds living then in Greece, the oracle declares, 'There is no one wiser than Socrates.' How amazed he must have been!

Socrates, who believed in dreams, signs and oracles, takes the answer seriously. He is a man 'called' to his mission, just as Moses and the Hebrew prophets were called by God to speak to the Jewish people. When I was first introduced to Socrates as a student I had a vague impression of him as an Old Testament kind of figure, and it was not just his beard and physical looks that fostered this resemblance. Like the prophets he is given a message to deliver to his people, whether they want to hear it or not. Socrates takes his mission from Apollo just as God appoints Jeremiah as his 'announcer to the nations':

> To whomever I shall send thee, thou shalt go; whatever I shall command thee, thou shalt speak. I have put my words in thy mouth; see, I appoint thee this day over the kingdoms, to root out, to tear down, to dismantle, to annihilate, to build, to plant.

The German-Jewish religious writer Martin Buber points out that the prophet's role is not primarily to predict what will happen but to confront people with the alternatives of decisions that are always available to them. There is real freedom of choice, the future is open, and it is the prophet's role to make people aware of the potential for disaster on one side and the possibility of salvation and return on the other,

> The prophet speaks the word that it is his task to speak; he is borne by this task, proceeding from a divine purpose and pointing to a divine goal. The spirit moves him; not only his organs of speech but the whole man is taken up in the service of the spirit. The body and life of the man become a part of this service and by this a symbol of the message.

This is the role that Socrates takes on, and his life becomes an example to his fellow Athenians, a model of the highest ethical teachings. Like the Hebrew prophets, his interests follow the teachings of the Torah,

Justice and justice only must you strive for.

Strangely enough, Socrates begins by testing the oracle, rather than just accepting it,

After contemplating the riddle for quite some time, I finally thought of a way to test its truth. I thought that if I could only find a man wiser than myself, then I could go back to the god with a clear refutation. I would say to the god, 'You said that I was the wisest man, but here is a person wiser than me.'

At the time of this experience, I was studying one of our famous politicians, Pericles, so I decided to start with him. When I began to question him, I could not help thinking that he was not really so wise, although many people thought he was, and Pericles himself thought he was extremely wise. I tried to explain to him that although he thought he was wise, that he really wasn't. Well, he didn't like to hear this, and the upshot was that he hated me, and his enmity was shared by all his friends who heard our conversation. So I left him, saying to myself, as I went away:

'Well, although I don't suppose either of us has any real knowledge to boast of, I am better off than he – for he knows nothing, but thinks that he does, whereas I am certain that I know nothing.'

In this way, it seemed I had a slight advantage over him, since at least I didn't think I knew what I really did not know.

And so Socrates started on his famous mission, a mission from the god Apollo to discover if there was someone wiser than himself,

Following this I questioned one man after another, always consciousness of the anger and hatred that I provoked, which distressed and alarmed me. But necessity drove me on – the word of God, I thought, must be considered first. So I said to myself, you must visit everyone who appears to know something, and discover the true meaning of the oracle. And I swear to you, fellow citizens, I swear! – for I must tell you the truth – the result of my mission was just this: I found that the men with the greatest reputation were almost always the most foolish; and some with no status at all were really wiser and better.

And after all of his discussions he came to this conclusion:

The real truth, Athenians, is that only God is wise; and by this oracle he wants to tell us that human wisdom is something completely insignificant. He is not speaking literally of Socrates, but is only using my name as an illustration, as if he were to say to us, 'The wisest of you mortals is one who, like Socrates, knows that his wisdom is in truth worth nothing.'

Socrates is not being ironic or falsely modest here, but there is a real humility to him. He understood that the greatest human knowledge is strictly limited when compared to the profound mysteries of life, where we find ourselves insignificant compared to the vastness of space and yet too large and clumsy to explore the infinitesimal atomic world. How can we ever know the answers to the really important questions: why are we here? How has life come about? What is consciousness, and where does it come from? A complete grasp of the nature of things is divine, not possible for mortals, who remain ignorant. Wisdom belongs only to the gods. And when we do acquire some knowledge it always seems to be accompanied by a dangerous pride and smugness. Bacon said, 'knowledge is power', and the power that knowledge gives us over nature and other people expands the ego in an unhealthy way; It creates in us an illusion of the grandiose, and may well lead us to destruction. Every gain in knowledge seems to give us a greater capacity for self-destruction.

Keeping a humble view of his own accomplishments meant that Socrates' mind remained alive in old age, open to new ideas and new experiences. He was willing to entertain doubts about his own knowledge of the world and to honestly accept the facts of his own ignorance. He saw knowledge as a living, interactive process, in which the truth must be pursued rather than discovered, and he was prepared to discard an older truth if an emergent new truth proved itself more apt. This is why he was so attractive to the young men who flocked to him.

This conversion from natural philosopher and scientist to ethical philosopher and seeker after wisdom is accompanied by other significant changes to his life. By the time he died, aged seventy, he had acquired a wife, Xanthippe, and three sons, the eldest sixteen and the youngest a toddler. This marriage took place when Socrates was in his early fifties and may reflect both his realisation that his life was moving towards its end and a desire to have progeny to carry on his name. In the *Symposium*, Plato's account of a drinking party that took place in 416 BCE, when Socrates was fifty-three, he gives the philosopher a speech about Eros (love) that shows this concern with both procreativity and immortality.

Socrates tells the assembled drinkers that he learned about Eros from a woman called Diotima, and he relates what she taught him:

> *'What kind of being is Eros, Diotima?' I asked.*
>
> *'He is a great spirit, Socrates, and like all spirits he is half god and half mortal.'*
>
> *'And what,' I said, 'is his function?'*
>
> *'He interprets,' she replied, 'between gods and people, conveying messages to the gods from the prayers and sacrifices of mortals, and giving to people the commands and*

replies of the gods; he is the mediator who spans the chasm that divides them, and he binds them altogether. God does not mingle with people except through Eros, and all the relations of god with people, whether awake or asleep, is carried on by Eros. The wisdom that understands this is spiritual; all other wisdom, such as that of arts and handicrafts, is mean and vulgar.'

The highest wisdom is spiritual wisdom, the only wisdom capable of understanding the spirit that is Love. Diotima goes on to ask Socrates how the function of Love expresses itself in action? When he cannot answer she gives him the meaning, one that relates closely to his own situation at this time:

'Eros's function is that of the procreation in what is beautiful, and this procreation can be either spiritual or physical . . . there is something divine about the whole matter; in procreation and bringing to birth the mortal creature is endowed with a touch of immortality . . . The object of Eros, Socrates, is not as you think, beauty.'
'What is it then?'
'Eros's object is to procreate and bring forth in beauty. Procreation is the nearest thing to perpetuity and immortality that a mortal can attain.

Socrates' late marriage and his desire for children could well be an expression of his need to find a form of immortality. Diotima's explanation tells us that if you truly feel the force of love in your life, even with the world's ugliness and brutality, then you are able, in whatever you do, to procreate what is beautiful. To be possessed by love is a divine gift, since love is a divine power. In a world where we find it difficult to express love, where it is often actively repressed, and easily replaced with indifference and heartlessness, this teaching is of the utmost importance.

9

THE HUMBLING
OF THE ATHENIAN
EMPIRE

Socrates was born during the glory days of classical Athens, in the fifth century BCE, and he lived through its eventual decline and failure. Because its history is also his history, and his death was an outcome of the tragic unravelling of the Athenian empire, I'm going to spend some time detailing these events.

The young, free and independent democracy that had defeated the Persians grew prosperous through international trade, and with its allied city-states and colonies in the Eastern Mediterranean, the Delian League, it gradually transformed itself into a maritime empire. The tribute paid by the allies into the Athenian treasury, the benefits of trade, and the rich silver mines controlled by Athens (and worked by slaves) made the city-state wealthy, and enabled its citizens to be paid a salary for attending assembly meetings and jury duty. This wealth created leisure time for the Athenian citizens, in which drama, music and philosophy flourished, and Athens became the cultural centre of Greece that Pericles had dreamed of.

The growing might of the Athenian empire inevitably brought it into conflict with Sparta, the other great Greek power, which also had its allies, the Peloponnesian League. The clash between these two empires, one based on sea power and the other on land, one a democracy and the other ruled by an oligarchy, broke out into open warfare in 431 BCE. This was the start of the Peloponnesian War, which was to last for twenty-seven years, and lead to a humiliating defeat for Athens, with the tearing down of her defensive walls and the loss of her democracy.

When the war began, the visionary Pericles was still the Athenian leader and general. He felt that Athens could win the war if it maintained a defensive strategy, bringing the outlying rural and country population within the city walls, and allowing the Spartan army to ravage the countryside, but do no real damage. As long as Athens had access to the sea and did not try to expand her empire during this time, he felt that they could not be defeated by a land army.

But Thucydides, who took part in the war as a general on the Athenian side and wrote a contemporary history of the conflict, makes the point that once the dogs of war are unleashed, there is a strong element of chance and contingency that no amount of planning can take into account, and calamities happen that no one can foresee:

Wide areas were affected by earthquakes; there were more eclipses of the sun than had ever been recorded before; in various parts of the country there were extensive droughts followed by famine; and there was the plague which did more harm and destroyed more life than almost any single factor. All these calamities fell together upon the Greeks after the war broke out.

After one year of war, a catastrophic plague descended on Athens and killed off one quarter of its population. The plague brought on despair, hopelessness, and lawlessness. When the plague returned again the next year, it claimed Pericles as one of its victims. Now a younger generation of men sought the leadership, men who had never fought in war and who were attracted by the desire for personal glory, fame, profit and action. They led the city-state into a more expansive and aggressive war policy than Pericles had advised and this eventually led to the Sicilian expedition, when an entire Athenian army and fleet were destroyed. Like modern-day Americans, most of the Athenians who voted to expand the war into Sicily probably had no idea where the island was, what military and economic power it had, or what dangers the strategy held. Euripides, who opposed the injustice and brutality of the war prophesied:

> *The rising generation shall lay their city in the dust.*
> *This is the inescapable truth.*

War itself was the greatest plague to hit Athens, attacking not just bodies, but corrupting souls as well. The war brought on a grave moral and religious crisis, which altered the ethical code of the city. There is a spiritual cost to be paid for any war, and no one knows the effect that a war will have on the souls of a country's people, especially when mass slaughter of the innocent occurs. In the Peloponnesian War there were a number of disturbing incidents involving colonies who attempted to break away from Athens and join Sparta. These small revolts were always heavily crushed by Athens, which could not afford to lose allies or their tribute, and when the breakaway colonies were defeated, retribution was always violent. In 416, the Athenians annihilated the small island-state of Melos when it refused to join the empire. They killed all the men of military age and sold into slavery the women and children, acts of terrible brutality and genocide. And this is only one example of a number of dubious victories over small states. Thucydides explained the loss of decency and humanity:

> *In times of peace and prosperity cities and individuals alike*
> *follow higher standards, because they are not forced into a*
> *situation where they have to do what they do not want to do.*
> *But war is a stern teacher; in depriving them of the power of*

easily satisfying their daily wants, it brings most people's minds down to the level of their actual circumstances.

A nation that uses force to take or keep an empire is always in danger of damaging and corrupting its collective soul, and Athens showed this degeneration of spirit as the war dragged on. Jacob Burckhardt said that power is in itself evil; that is, Martin Buber claims, 'when it wills itself, when it resists the spirit, when power takes possession of those who use it, penetrates them and permeates them with the drive for power for itself.' During the long war, Athens abandoned the high ideals of humanity that its poets, artists and philosophers had created. Loved for her virtue and beauty, Athens became sour and harsh, and lost her sense of justice. She had to understand and come to terms with defeat and loss, her people demoralised and poor.

After twenty-seven years of war, Sparta defeated Athens, dismantled her navy, took away her overseas possessions, her mines and defences, and set up an oligarchy of thirty men to rule. But the oligarchy was so vicious and unpopular that it became known as the Thirty Tyrants, and after only three years of a reign of terror a popular democracy rose up in civil war, with the aim of seizing power and resurrecting the empire. At the very end of the century, almost as the last gasp of a dying culture, the exhausted, defeated, war-ravaged Athenians brought Socrates to court on charges of impiety and corrupting the young.

Although the restored democracy had declared an amnesty for all crimes committed before 403 BCE, three citizens came forward to condemn Socrates in what I can only assume was a political/religious show trial, an act of revenge against a political dissident. There is no historical evidence of a specific reason for this trial, but many commentators feel that it is an act of retribution for Socrates' influence on men who became oligarchs and enemies of the democracy. E.R. Dodds comments:

But the evidence we have is more than enough to prove that the Great Age of Greek Enlightenment was also, like our own time, an age of Persecution.

He goes on to explain why at this period a charge of irreligion was so often selected as the surest means of suppressing an unwelcome voice or damaging a political opponent:

Important was the influence of wartime hysteria. If we allow for the fact that wars cast their shadows before them and leave emotional disturbances behind them, the Age of Persecution coincides pretty closely with the longest and most disastrous war in Greek history.

Dodds quotes R. Crawshay-Williams who, in *The Comforts of Unreason*, observed that, 'in times of danger to the community the whole tendency to conformity is greatly strengthened: the herd huddles together and becomes more intolerant than ever of "cranky" opinion.'

Certainly no opinion was crankier than Socrates'. He was most likely prosecuted for being a dissident, for publicly speaking his mind. Perhaps the Athenians no longer wanted to hear criticism of their war policies, and were willing to kill the spirit that their own highest ideals had created. A democracy's greatest danger is when the people themselves curtail their own freedom.

Socrates was a loyal Athenian, who fought as a soldier in several battles, took office when he was called on, but who studiously avoided politics and public life. In this, he was unlike most Athenians. At his trial he said:

Can you really imagine my surviving into old age if I had led a public life, conducting myself like an honourable man in what was right, and making justice, as I should, the most important thing? No, indeed, Athenians, neither I nor any other man would have lived long. But I have always been consistent in all my actions, public as well as private. I have never approved any action incompatible with justice on the part of anyone, including those who are maliciously called my disciples. The person who conscientiously opposes the will of the people, honestly struggling against illegalities and wrongs taking place, will not be able to preserve his life. The person who is a true champion of justice, if he wants to survive even for a short time, must combat injustice privately and leave politics alone.

We can assume from this comment that Socrates would not have found the war policy and genocide of the Athenian empire to his liking. But this shows the downside to the search for a living truth. In his philosophical search Socrates discovered higher values of political justice and religious respect than were acceptable in his time. Because philosophy is a totality, an attitude towards everything, every philosophy must also encompass a religion and a political theory. It is easy to see that Socrates' philosophy and his ensuing attitudes to religion and politics would come into conflict with the prevailing attitudes of his day. Anyone who engages in an objective, rational search for the truth will always come into conflict with the political, religious and financial interests of the authorities who are happier with their own limited and biased versions of the truth.

The official Athenian religion was purely ritualistic, requiring sacrifices at specific times to mollify the gods and to ensure their help for Athens; it had no emotional or spiritual aspect. In political life, justice was a highly elastic concept, often stretched to sanctify unjust acts. A critical intelligence sitting in judgement of the unreflective traditional social order was a threat to the *polis*. The power of the state to manipulate public opinion through the media means that their version of the truth will normally prevail, as it did in Socrates' trial in 399 BCE.

Whether Socrates made his opposition plain in his discussions in the streets we do not know, but he always made it clear that he was no admirer of democracy. He believed that the best rulers could not be chosen by lot, as the Athenians chose their assembly members, but considered statesmanship or leadership as another form of knowledge, a type of *aretē* or excellence, which was partly an inherent skill but which had to be trained and developed.

In Athens this was a non-democratic idea, since the Athenian democracy was built on the belief that the people themselves, meeting together, discussing issues and voting as a collective, would make the correct decision enough times to enable society to run properly. Since the men who voted were also the ones who manned the ships during war, it was assumed that they would pursue what they saw as their self-interest in the Assembly. In cases where this self-interest led to conflict with other states, they would be the ones who would have to defend their views with their lives.

Socrates did not believe that either the many, the people acting as a collective, or the few, the small group of wealthy landowners and aristocrats, could make the best decisions for the state. When the few, the oligarchy, managed to wrest power from the people the results were disastrous, and showed that when a small group seized power they could be even more corrupt and venal than the democracy. Instead, Socrates said that the best person, the expert, the one who showed the finest *aretē*, goodness or excellence for the task, should be appointed for it. Of course, Socrates never set up a system to show how this person could be found or placed in power, so his ideas were purely theoretical. It was left to Plato in the *Republic* to work out such a system of rulership.

In practice Socrates followed the laws of his city even though he did not like the way it was governed. No doubt his vocal insistence that this was the case led his fellow citizens to understand that he was not in sympathy with their delibera- tions and actions, and this must have created a prejudice against him in the eyes of most Athenians. The ensuing trial and death of Socrates was a clear emblem of Athenian decline.

10

THE TRIAL

There's a limit to life, but to knowledge there's no limit.
Using what's limited to seek out the unlimited is futile.
And if, knowing this, we still act according to knowledge,
then danger can't be avoided.   CHUANG TZU

The seventy-year-old Socrates was brought to court in 399 BCE by three accusers, Anytus, Melytus and Lycon, and the accusations were that he ignored the gods that the state recognised, introduced new gods of his own devising, and corrupted the young of Athens. These charges, although real, seem to be only a pretext for two more fundamental though hidden charges: that Socrates, a sceptic about democracy, taught people like Alcibiades and Critias, who became oligarchs and enemies of the Athenian democracy, and that he was critical of the injustices and brutality perpetrated by the Athenians in the war. He was being prosecuted for his supposed influence on other people and for his opinions and public discussions.

The trial took place in an open-air court in front of a jury of five hundred Athenian citizens chosen by lot and it lasted for the customary one day. First, the three accusers each related one of the charges, and the main accuser, Meletus, finished by asking for the death penalty. Scholars agree that the trial was an attempt to silence the critical and dissident philosopher, so the aim of the trial may have been to force Socrates into exile. But he decided that he would give up his life if he couldn't live as he wished, rather than save his skin by leaving the country.

Although Socrates made a defence speech it is not a very spirited defence against the charges but rather a speech defending himself as a philosopher. In it he describes how Aristophanes' comedy *Clouds* slandered him, he talks about his mission, and explains that rather than corrupt the young, he is the one person who was trying to help and educate them. After his speech he was found guilty by a majority of thirty votes. Socrates now had a second chance to address the jury, to discuss the punishment. From his point of view he had done nothing wrong, and was not guilty, so what punishment did he deserve? He cheekily asked that the punishment be free meals for life at the Pyrtaneum, the banqueting hall where former Olympic champions were fed at the state's expense. The second vote went more badly for him, an increased majority of eighty, which confirmed the death penalty, administered by drinking hemlock, a poison.

It is deeply ironic that a person of such intense religious and spiritual feeling as Socrates was found guilty of impiety. It is probably true that he did not believe in the state gods, but he was not alone; many people, and not just philosophers, had questioned the existence of the gods. But even with this disbelief Xenophon tells us that Socrates performed the ritual sacrifices regularly, and did not ignore his religious duties. The charge that he introduced new gods relates to his oracle or inner sign. Although Athens believed in free speech it would not tolerate someone who held his own inner spirit higher than the state's morality. The inner sign was always the highest authority for Socrates; if it could speak to him then other people might begin to tune into their own inner voices, and it would be dangerous for the state if people opened themselves to the kind of life in which this inner voice could be heard and trusted.

Socrates trusts enough in his inner voice to rely on it at

the trial for his most important decision: the choice of his own death, which he now sees in a positive light:

> Till now my inner oracle has constantly been in the habit of opposing me even about trivial things, if I was about to make a mistake or error. Now, as you can see, something has happened which may be thought, and is generally believed to be, the final and worst evil, but my oracle gave me no sign of opposition, either as I was leaving my house this morning, or when I was going into the court, or at any point in my speech. The oracle has often stopped me in the middle of a sentence, but this time it has not opposed anything I either said or did.
>
> I regard this as proof that what has happened to me is in fact a blessing, and that we're mistaken in thinking that death is an evil. I have good grounds for saying this, for if the way I handled my case was not going to bring some good result the sign would surely have stopped me.

Concluding from this that death as well as life is a gift and a blessing, Socrates repeats one of his famous paradoxes, that a good person cannot be harmed either in life or in death:

> I want you to be aware that if you kill someone like me, you will injure yourselves much more than you will injure me, because I do not believe that the law of god permits a better man to be harmed by a worse. I do not deny that a bad man may put a good man to death, or drive him into exile, or deprive him of his civil rights. They and others may imagine that these are great evils, but I do not agree with them. I believe that to do what Anytus is doing – trying to take away an innocent man's life – is a far greater evil.

That nothing can harm the good person is a religious conception of philosophy, and therefore must be taken as a matter of faith. Socrates believes that misfortunes cannot harm a good person's soul or character, because no matter what calamity befalls a person the only matter of importance is the state of his or her soul. If he has attained his own proper *aretē*, his excellence as a human being, then evil cannot harm him.

Socrates, in keeping with his high ideals of non-violence and non-harm, forgives his accusers and the jury for having committed this injustice against him:

Therefore, my judges, take death lightly, and know this as a truth – that nothing can harm a good man, either in life or after death, and his fortunes are not neglected by the gods. My own approaching end has not happened by mere chance. I see clearly that to die and to be released from my mission was really better for me, and that is why my sign never turned me back. This is also why I am not angry with my accusers or my judges; they have not done me any real harm, although it wasn't with any kind intention that they did so, but because they thought they were harming me; and that is something for which I can gently blame them.

Socrates opposed the *lex talionis* (an eye for an eye) and popular ideas of revenge and retribution; he held a rarefied view of aggression and violence that has been shared by very few people in history, but most famously by Rabbi Jesus, and more recently by Mahatma Gandhi and the Dalai Lama. He believed that in all cases it was wrong to do evil, because of the harm this would inflict on your soul. Even when wronged, we must never retaliate, because this would only trade evil for evil and escalate the wrong. As they say, 'An eye for an eye and the whole world will be blind', since violence repaid for violence leads to an endless cycle of evil. This dialogue is from the *Crito*:

SOCRATES: *Are we to remain assured, in spite of the opinion of the many, and in spite of the consequences whether better or worse, of the truth of what we said, that injustice is always an evil and dishonour to the person who acts unjustly? Can we affirm that?*

CRITO: *Yes.*

SOCRATES: *Then we must not do wrong?*

CRITO: *Certainly not.*

SOCRATES: *Not even if injured to commit an injury in return, which is how most people think; we must never injure anyone at all?*

CRITO: *Clearly not.*

SOCRATES: *Again, Crito, should we do evil?*

CRITO: *Surely not, Socrates.*

SOCRATES: *And what about doing evil in return for evil, which is the morality of the many – is that just or not?*

CRITO: *Not just.*

SOCRATES: *Because doing evil to another person is the same as injuring him?*

CRITO: *Very true.*

SOCRATES: *Then we should not retaliate or exchange evil for evil to anyone, whatever evil we may have suffered from them. For this opinion has never been held, and never will be held, by a large number of people; and those who agree and disagree about this point have no common ground, and can only despise one another, when they see how widely they differ. For this has always been, and is still, my opinion;*

The golden rule, to treat others as you would like to be treated, is the first, the simplest and the most obvious law of ethics and spirituality. It is the basis of fairness and justice, and enables us to live together in peace through respect for our common humanity. It is also the first law that we abandon when we grow up since it clashes with the selfish values of our competitive market-led society. To his credit, Socrates never grew out of it, but upheld it in his life and work, and paid for his beliefs with his death. To unswervingly follow the path of truth, no matter how difficult or dangerous that path becomes, shows the mark of a truly great and unique person.

11

DEATH BY POISON

Socrates was now taken from the court to the cells, and would have died the following day, but the occurrence of a religious holiday meant that no execution could take place, and the philosopher had to wait a month in jail. He spent this time in discussions with his friends, associates and family, many of whom were with him when he was given the hemlock by the jailer. This is how Plato describes the scene in the *Phaedo*:

Now the hour of sunset was near . . . the prison officer walked into the room and said to him, 'Socrates, since you are the noblest, gentlest and best of all the men who ever came here, I am sure you will not get angry with me like the others, who raged and swore at me when, in obedience to the magistrates, I told them to drink the poison. I am sure you will not be angry with me because it is others, and not I, who are responsible for this. You know what I must do now, so try to bear lightly what you must endure.' Then saying goodbye, he burst into tears, turned away and went out.

Socrates looked at his departing figure and said, 'I return your good wishes, and will do as you bid.' Then, turning to us, he said, 'How charming the man is: since I have been in prison he has been coming to see me, and at times he would talk to me, and was as good as could be to me, and now see how generously he grieves for me. But we must do as he says, Crito; let the cup be brought, if the poison is prepared: if not, let the attendant prepare some.'

'But,' said Crito, 'the sun is still above the hilltops, and many have taken the poison late, and even after the announcement was made, have eaten and drunk, and enjoyed themselves; there is still time, do not hurry.'

Socrates said, 'Crito, they may have been right in doing this, for they thought that they would gain by the delay; but I am right in not doing it this way, for I do not think that I shall gain anything by drinking the poison a little later; I would just be sparing and saving a life which is already gone, and I could only laugh at myself for this. Please do as I say, and don't refuse me.'

Crito, when he heard this, made a sign to the servant, and the servant went in, and remained for some time, and then returned with the jailer carrying a cup of poison. Socrates said, 'You, my good friend, who are experienced in these matters, give me directions as to how I am to proceed.' The man answered, 'You have only to walk around until your legs get heavy, and then lie down, and the poison will act.' He handed the cup to Socrates, who in the easiest and gentlest manner, without the least fear or change of colour or feature, looking directly at the man as his manner was, took the cup and said, 'What do you say about making a libation out of this cup to a god? May I, or not?' The man answered, 'We only prepare, Socrates, just as much as we think will be enough.'

'I understand,' he said. 'Yet I may and must pray to the gods to prosper my journey from this to that other world. May this, which is my prayer, be granted to me.'

Then, holding the cup to his lips, quite readily and cheerfully he drank the poison. Up to now most of us had been able to control our sorrow; but now when we saw him drinking, and saw too that he had drained the cup, we could no longer contain ourselves, and in spite of myself my own tears were flowing fast. I covered my face and wept over myself, for certainly I was not weeping over him, but at the thought of my own calamity in having lost such a companion. Nor was I the first, for Crito, when he found himself unable to restrain his tears, had got up and moved away, and I followed; and at that moment. Apollodorus, who had been weeping all the time, broke out in a loud cry which made cowards of us all. Socrates alone retained his calmness,

'What is this strange outcry? I sent the women away so they might not offend in this way, for I have heard that a man should die in peace. Be quiet, then, and have patience.'

When we heard that, we were ashamed, and held back our tears, and he walked some more until, as he said, his legs began to fail, and then he lay on his back, and the man who gave him the poison now and then looked at his feet and legs; and after a while he pressed his foot hard and asked him if he could feel; and he said, no; and then his leg, and so upwards and upwards, and showed us that he was cold and stiff. And he felt them himself, and said:

'When the poison reaches the heart, that will be the end.'

He was beginning to grow cold around his groin, when he uncovered his face, for he had covered himself up, and said (and they were his last words) – he said:

'Crito, I owe a cock to Asclepius. Will you remember to pay the debt?'

'The debt shall be paid,' said Crito. 'Is there anything else?'

There was no answer to this question; but in a minute or two a movement was heard, and the attendants uncovered him. His eyes were set, and Crito closed his eyes and mouth.

Such was the end of our friend, whom I may truly call the wisest, and justest, and best of all the men whom I have ever known.

As an epitaph let us reflect on Buber's thoughts on the prophet's role,

The prophet fails in the hour of history, but not in so far as the future of his people is concerned. The prophetic spirit does not succeed in giving the reality of its hour what it wills to give it. But it instils the vision in the people for all time to come. It lives within the people from then on as a longing to realize the truth.

12

PLATO AND XENOPHON

After Socrates' death a minor industry developed in books of memoirs, dialogues and stories about him. We have some fragments from his close associate, Aeschines, but the substantial writings that remain are the many dialogues of Plato, and the *Memorabilia* of Xenophon. Plato did not begin to write about his teacher immediately on his death but waited for ten years, until around 390 BCE, before writing the *Apology*, the earliest of his works. We are not sure when Xenophon wrote his work but it was probably after Plato, since the former military commander wrote only in his retirement.

Scholars find it disconcerting that the Socrates portrayed in Plato and Xenophon differ so much in their character and philosophical interests. Plato's Socrates is a complex, subtle and ironic seeker after the truth, a rationally-minded man who professes personal ignorance and is trying to obtain secure knowledge from others. In his search for wisdom he asks questions about the most important ideas and values of life – justice, self-control, happiness and so on.

Xenophon's Socrates, a completely different kind of person, appears to be made of wisdom, and is forever giving people advice about how to conduct their affairs. He is a warm, avuncular character, deeply knowledgeable about everything, and when asked questions by others is very happy to volunteer pedestrian morality and dull sermons. Xenophon's dialogues are sometimes in the same form as Plato's (the *elenchus* or dialectical method of question and answer) but are more often reports of conversations that Socrates had with Xenophon and others.

Why is there this profound difference? I think the answer lies partly in Socrates and partly in the differing characters and interests of Plato and Xenophon. Socrates had many followers and after his death a number of them set up their own schools of philosophy. Plato, Aristippus, Antisthenes and Euclides all claimed that Socrates was their mentor, yet their philosophies are completely at odds with each others'. Plato set up an idealistic system based on the idea that there is a perfect reality above the world of the senses that we can only reach through a denial of the world of sense. Aristippus believed that philosophical happiness could only be reached by a wholehearted pursuit of physical pleasure, by a constant pursuit of desires. Antisthenes believed the exact opposite, that happiness could only be found by an ascetic reduction of desires. Euclides was inspired by Socrates' love of discussion to found a school of logical argumentation.

How could each student claim to be the true follower of Socrates, and yet be so divergent in their beliefs? It appears that each one had a different view of Socrates and what he taught, and they each took from him a different perspective, partly based on their own interests. But it may also be that Socrates directed his talks with each of these men in a way that suited their interests and needs at the time. His philosophy was not a 'one size fits all' approach, a given system that everyone had to subscribe to, but a vision of life, a set of values that could be applied in many different ways. His teaching was a living process, a series of discussions that he could adjust to the levels of his listeners and co-speakers.

We can see a similar approach in the ancient Chan (Zen) Buddhist stories. The original Buddhists in India had relied on meditation and study of the scriptures as a slow and steady path to enlightenment, but not everyone became enlightened through this method. When Buddhism was transplanted to

China, they developed a new approach to enlightenment – the *sudden* approach, which did not rely on intellectual methods. The old Zen Masters used many different methods to bring their young monks to enlightenment depending on their capacity, level of interest and personal type. Some Masters used a loud shout to shock a monk into self-realisation, others used a sharp blow with a staff, while some used stories and sayings (koans) that could not be understood logically, to shake up the conditioned thinking of would-be adepts. There was a different mode of approach for each type of student.

This is not so different from the process that Plato describes in his Seventh Letter as his 'sudden' awakening to philosophy,

Acquaintance with it (philosophy) must come rather after a long period of attendance on instruction in the subject itself and of close companionship when, suddenly, like a blaze kindled by a leaping spark, it is generated in the soul and at once becomes self-sustaining.

If we compare Plato and Xenophon, we can see why Socrates would want and need to discuss different ideas with them. Plato was a highly intelligent, subtle and sensitive thinker, interested in philosophical ideas and how best to apply them to individuals and the state. He was an intellectual interested in working out a philosophical and social system that could be used to create the best possible government. Until Socrates' death, Plato had been planning a career as a statesman and politician, but he was so appalled by what happened to his mentor that he became a philosopher instead. You can understand why Socrates would happily discuss ideas with Plato, because that is what interested him, but not with Xenophon.

Xenophon was ambitious for a military career which could bring him glory and honour. Said to be very handsome, he was a more mundane thinker than Plato, and a much more physical person, enjoying riding horses and country living. He was interested in Socrates because he could learn from him, and obtain good advice, which he seems to have largely ignored. Xenophon, like Plato, was not in favour of democracy, and he especially admired the Spartan way of life, eventually fighting with Sparta against Athens, for which he was exiled. In his retirement in Sparta he became an historian, a rather poor one in comparison with Thucydides.

At the time of Socrates' death, Xenophon was twenty-seven, and Plato twenty-eight. Neither of them had known Socrates when he was young or middle-aged, but only as an old man. Because of their youth, they could not have spent that much time with him, and neither of them were part of the close inner circle of Socrates' associates. The fact that they were both writing from memory, at least a good ten years after the events they are reporting, must also make us aware that the Socrates they present is not only vastly different in each writer's case, but there is a strong possibility that poor recollection or just good imagination may have added a great deal of fictional elements to their factual reporting.

So this might be the answer as to why Socrates is so different to each writer. Socrates presented himself differently to each man, according to his reading of their interests and capacity, and each man viewed him from their own needs and point of view. Plato's Socrates is dominated by reason and philosophical discourse, while Xenophon's Socrates is a down-to-earth purveyor of wisdom.

DID SOCRATES
BELIEVE IN THE
IMMORTALITY OF
THE SOUL?

13

Many readers have been introduced to Socrates' trial and
death through the Penguin Classic *The Last Days Of
Socrates*, which is a compilation of four of Plato's dialogues
dealing with the philosopher's last days. The four dialogues:
Euthyphro, *Apology*, *Crito* and *Phaedo*, have a unity of time
and subject. They all take place within the last few weeks of
the philosopher's life and all deal with his trial and its outcome.
The *Euthyphro* is set just before the trial and its subject, piety,
concerns two of the charges brought against Socrates; the
Apology is the trial itself, the *Crito* takes place in prison and
deals with Socrates' decision not to escape, while the *Phaedo*
argues for the immortality of the soul and ends with Socrates'
death. The latter three all take place in the thirty-day period
from trial to death.

But this apparent unity is deceptive when we look at
Socrates' attitude to the life of the soul after death as expressed
in these dialogues. There is a marked difference between his
early view at the trial and the later one in the *Phaedo*. In the
Apology he states that there are two possibilities for the soul
after death: either complete unconsciousness and annihilation
of body and soul together or the transmigration of his soul

to join all the other dead souls in the underworld Hades. He does not stake an opinion about which one he believes will happen to him or seem terribly concerned about either option, but considers both of them blessings,

> *If we reflect on this in another way we shall see that there is much reason to hope that death is a blessing. Death is one of two things – either it's a state of utter annihilation and complete unconsciousness, or, as most people believe, it's a migration of the soul from this world to another.*
>
> *Now if you suppose that in death there is no consciousness, but only a deep sleep undisturbed even by dreams, that would be a priceless gain. If you were to select the night in which you slept so soundly as to not even dream, and were to compare this with all the other nights of your life, and then were told to say how many nights you had passed in your entire life more pleasantly than this one, I don't think that anyone, not even the great King Of Persia, would find many such nights, when compared with the others. Now if death is like this, I say that to die is a blessing; for eternity can then be regarded as no more than a single night.*
>
> *But if death is a journey to another place, and all the dead are there, as people think, what blessing, my friends and judges, can be greater than this?*

However, in the *Phaedo* Socrates believes very strongly that the soul is immortal and lives on after death, and he argues this point passionately and intensely.

> *We admitted that everything living is born of the dead. For if the soul existed before birth, and in coming to life and being born can be born only from death and dying, must she not after death continue to exist, since she has to be born again? Surely the proof which you desire has been already furnished.*
>
> *The soul is in the very likeness of the divine, and immortal, and intelligible, and uniform, and indissoluble, and unchange-*

able; and the body is in the very likeness of the human, and mortal, and unintelligible, and multiform, and dissoluble, and changeable. Can this be denied?

That soul, I say, herself invisible, departs to the invisible World to the divine and immortal and rational: arriving, she lives in bliss and is released from the error and folly of men, their fears and wild passions and all other human ills, and forever dwells, as they say of the initiated, in company with the gods.

When I first read the *Phaedo* years ago this difference did not bother me, but rereading it I was struck by how divergent the two views are, and I actually found it difficult to finish reading the *Phaedo* because I felt that this was not Socrates speaking, or at least not the Socrates of the *Apology*. The question that I had was, how could he have made such a quantum jump in his thinking in such a brief time? Of course, radical change of mind is possible, but if Socrates had experienced such an important change in such a short time, surely he would have mentioned this fact to his companions in the *Phaedo* itself. Instead, he argues as if the immortality of the soul is his long-established view. The puzzle resolved itself when I read some essays by the late, great, classical scholar Gregory Vlastos, who gave the reasons for this radical sea change.

Vlastos explains that the *Apology*, *Crito* and *Euthyphro* are all early dialogues of Plato, dialogues in which he tries to capture the character, activities and thought of his beloved teacher, whereas the *Phaedo* is a much later dialogue, written when Plato had developed his own ideas and philosophy, but continued to use Socrates as a mouthpiece. So divergent did these ideas become that the nineteenth-century Russian scholar Solovyov made the point that the state proposed by Plato in his late dialogue, *Laws*, would have rejected a free spirit like Socrates.

This is why I felt such a dislocation between the *Phaedo* and the others, and as I read more I realised that Plato's work contains at least two divergent attitudes to the soul, one from the early dialogues that we can call Socratic and which may be original to Socrates, and another from the later dialogues that we can call Platonic, and is probably derived from Pythagorean philosophy, a later influence on Plato. Why should readers today be concerned about the difference between these two attitudes to the soul, expressed by two ancient thinkers? The reason is that ideas have power, words have abiding influence, and Plato's conception of the soul has had a great influence on our western conception of reality, an influence that has been both bad and good. There is nothing wrong with believing in an immortal soul, and it is a comforting thought to those who believe in it, but I don't believe that Socrates, on the evidence in the *Apology*, believed in his soul's immortality.

However, the real problem doesn't lie in whether one believes or disbelieves in the immortality of the soul, but in the ramifications that follow from the initial premise. Plato identifies the human soul exclusively with its moral and intellectual aspects, a view which sees a person as a composite, with body and soul in distinct, separate compartments, working together, but not as an integrated unity. Like Socrates, Plato considers the spirit as the essence of humanity, but unlike Socrates, he sees the body as a prison which stops the spirit from departing this corrupt world of appearances for the ideal world of reality that Plato believed existed beyond it. This ideal world was a changeless, eternal realm, a place where mathematical forms expressed the highest truth, and this supernatural place was for Plato the true home of the spirit. In the *Phaedo*, Plato describes how, at the point of death, the soul would gather itself together in the body to make that journey:

> And what is purification but the separation of the soul from the body; (at death) the habit of the soul gathering and collecting herself into herself, out of all the parts of the body and dwelling

*in her own place alone, as in another life, so also in this one,
as far as she can; the release of the soul from the chains of
the body.*

Plato's view of the soul was entirely different from any earlier
Greek conception. The Greek word *psyche*, or spirit, which
is usually translated as 'soul', originally meant the physical
breath which gives us life, and this is how it was seen in
Homer, as the life-breath, similar to the Chinese *chi* and the
Indian *prana*. *Psyche* is not really the soul but *life* or the *cause
of life*, and in a human being its activities include sensation
and perception, emotion and thought. As breath the *psyche*
permeates the body with which it is totally blended, giving
life and warmth, growth and maintenance. Since *psyche* and
body are one, and it is the breath that links them together
there is a natural unity to the living person.

The early Greeks experienced through their senses this
immediate reality of the world. D.H. Lawrence describes
imaginatively how ancient cultures perceive the world:

*In the oldest religion everything was alive, not supernaturally
but naturally alive. There were only deeper and deeper streams
of life, vibrations of life, more and more vast. So rocks were
alive, but a mountain had a deeper vaster life than a rock, and
it was much harder for a man to bring his spirit, or his energy,
into contact with the life of the mountain . . . For the whole life
effort of man was to get his life into direct contact with the
elemental life of the cosmos, mountain-life, cloud-life, thunder-
life, air-life, earth-life, sun-life. To come into immediate felt
contact and so derive energy, power and a dark sort of joy.*

To the early Greeks reality was full of life and spirit and there
was no reason to consider differences between matter and
mind or body and soul. Everything in the universe was
connected in a great unity, the divine and the mortal being
part of one continuous streaming universe. Socrates inherited

this view of reality and believed both the body and the spirit to be equally important for life on this earth. The Socratic conception of the total self implies a necessary relationship of soul and body, and not a split; the soul cannot function apart from bodily conditions of being.

14

SOCRATES' CONCEPTION OF THE SOUL

Socrates sees the self, the complete person, as a whole, self-regulating organism consisting of body and soul working together, a spiritual/physical totality. The body contains its sensations and impulses, while the soul is made up of two non-physical aspects: the mind with its thoughts, emotions and feelings, and the spirit, that silent internal witness or sign. All these parts are integrated into a unity, the subject of all the experiences of life – the self. In Socrates' view of the self the body is accepted as an integral part but is given an inferior role, since it is the rational mind that he considers the ruler of the whole. Body and mind are united, with the mind having control over the body's impulses. However, the highest authority, the ultimate ruler over all, is the inner spirit, the sign or oracle that Socrates always heeded. This spirit or guardian angel has the ultimate control over the total self, so there is a trinity in the soul or self: spirit, mind, body.

The Socratic soul does not lose touch with nature, and does not separate the mind from the instinctual and life-preserving impulses of the body. Because there is an intimate organic connection between what we sense, feel, think and know about the world and about ourselves, the simultaneous experiences of outer and inner life, there is a consequent feeling of oneness, of being at home on the earth. With this feeling of oneness, life has purpose and meaning, because we do not feel that we are merely disembodied souls forced to endure a corrupt physical life, but are creatures fully alive, able to interact freely with everyone and everything in our environment. To be in a state of positive health is to be on good terms with the universe. To create this state of well-being requires that we care for our total self, and for Socrates that includes caring not just for the soul but for the body. We know from Xenophon that Socrates believed it was necessary to exercise the body to keep it healthy and strong,

> *Don't you know that those who are physically weak can, by exercising their bodies, become stronger than those who neglect them, and can endure the effort of exercise with more comfort? And don't you think that I, who am constantly preparing my body by exercise to endure whatever may happen to it, bear everything more easily than you, who neglects all exercise?*

The gymnasia or sports grounds were among Socrates' favourite hangouts, and in Athens these were places not just of physical exercise but were also mind gyms, where ideas were freely discussed. His idea of health was a complete fitness of body and soul, which resulted from living fully the philosophical life.

The Socratic soul – mind and spirit operating together as one – is where we find the moral and ethical character of the person, and it is here that *aretē* (excellence or goodness) can be developed, since the soul is the homeland of *aretē*. To bring health and well-being to the self, the whole person, you need to bring health and well-being to the soul, and it is the rational self-control of the soul that secures the well-being of all. This relationship of soul and body was explained partly through a story Socrates tells in Plato's *Charmides*, where the young and beautiful Charmides is suffering from a headache and Socrates claims he has a cure:

> Our eminent physicians say to a patient who comes to them with bad eyes, that they cannot undertake to cure his eyes by themselves, but that if his eyes are to be cured, his head must be treated too. And then again they say that to think of curing the head alone, and not the rest of the body also, is the height of folly. And arguing in this way they apply their regime to the whole body, and try to heal the whole and the part together.
>
> The Greek physicians are quite right as far as they go, but Zalmoxis, the Thracian king, says that just as you ought not to attempt to cure the eyes without the head, or the head without the body, so neither ought you to attempt to cure the body without the soul. And this is the reason why the cure of many diseases is unknown to the Greek physicians, because they disregard the whole, which ought to be studied also, for the part can never be well unless the whole is well.
>
> For all good and evil, whether in the body or in the whole man, originates in the soul and flows from there, as if from the head to the eyes. And therefore if the head and body are to be well, you must begin by curing the soul – that is the first and essential thing. And the cure of the soul is to be effected by the use of certain charms, and these charms are beautiful words, and by them self-mastery and harmony are implanted in the soul, and where self-mastery comes and stays, there health is quickly imparted, not only to the head but to the whole body.

Socrates understood all about psychosomatic illness, that mind and body are so fully integrated that either has the power to create illness or health in the other, without an outside cause. His understanding is that the soul can be improved or made more excellent by doing right, and this advances its *aretē*, or the excellence or goodness of the self. In the *Crito* he explains that injustice in the soul is like a fatal disease in the body. The health and well-being of the body is strongly influenced by the positive nature of the thoughts of the mind,

SOCRATES: *If, acting under the advice of men who have no understanding, we destroy what can be improved by health and degraded by disease – (And here I mean the body) – when that has been destroyed, would life be worth having?*
CRITO: *No.*
SOCRATES: *Could we live, having an evil and corrupted body?*
CRITO: *Certainly not.*
SOCRATES: *And will life be worth having, if the higher part of man, the part that is improved by justice and degraded by injustice, becomes corrupted? Do we consider this principle, whatever it may be in man, that has to do with justice and injustice, to be inferior to the body?*
CRITO: *Certainly not.*
SOCRATES: *In fact more honoured?*
CRITO: *Much more honoured.*

Although there is a distinction between the higher part of the self (the soul) and the lower self (the body), there is no doubt that both parts are unified in the person, and this kind of view makes certain that the body is not dismissed as a degraded prison or cage for the pristine soul. In Socrates' conception of the human soul, matter would be full of spirit, and spirit embedded in matter, and so both would be sacred and holy. This kind of integrated relationship between spirit and matter, between the self and the world, inner and outer, reflects the way that Eastern religions have always perceived of life, as we in the West are now beginning to do.

There is an enormous gulf between life as experienced by the integrated and holistic Socratic self, which combines body, mind and spirit into an organic whole, a complete unified person, and that of the Platonic soul, which claims that the rational, thinking part is of an essentially divine and separate nature. It seems obvious that as Plato developed his own philosophy he moved away from Socrates' idea of the integrated soul and body in the real world to a vision of reality in another incorporeal realm. Of the two I believe that the integrated and holistic Socratic soul reflects human experience better, is healthier, more life-affirming, and ties in with contemporary views of science and psychology.

15

HOW WE LOST
OUR SOULS

The argument I am proposing is that Socrates held a holistic view of the self, but because Plato developed his own independent views, Socrates' integrated model was effectively buried and lost, leaving the heavily spiritualised Platonic version to become the Western model. It is Plato's version of Socrates' ideas that has inspired the Western mind. This has led to an unbalanced and distorted view of human life that has initiated literally centuries of sexual frustration and suffering and has led in recent times to the industrial pollution of the Earth on a scale that now threatens human existence.

Partly because of Plato we have learned to live in the head, and have lost touch with the body, and in particular with the heart, the site of our deepest feelings. Our relationship to nature has been fragmented, and the resulting heartlessness of our societies, the constant push for ever-increasing wealth and power through aggressive trade policies and wars, has resulted in a loss of health and well-being that has put our continued existence into question.

I don't mean to blame Plato for this. He merely transmitted his ideas to his students, but the influence of these ideas, once they were taken up, absorbed, and reinterpreted by Christianity and then developed and elaborated by thinkers like Bacon, Descartes and Newton became the foundation for our Western view of the world, and indirectly led to our current crisis.

The Platonic concept of the separation of the immortal soul from the corrupt body was shoehorned into the Christian soul, which gave the church a grudging toleration of sexuality and a particularly negative approach to women. The celibate St Paul was afraid of the body and of sexuality, especially female sexuality, and was happy to base the new Christian religion on a spiritual basis, denigrating the body and its needs.

Over time, the effect of considering body and soul as different entities led to a complete conceptual split of the human being. At the beginning of the seventeenth century Descartes declared 'cogito ergo sum' – I do not doubt my existence since I think – identifying his being with the thinking part of himself. He tried to find an order in life, not through unifying it but by dividing it, and he partitioned the universe into a triangle of I-World-God which made God (the spirit) completely separate both from the world and from the 'I'. Instead of the spiritual infusing the world, and the ego (the 'I') involved in both the world and the spirit, we are left with an ego alone and isolated, looking out on a soulless world. All of our intuitive and instinctive qualities were separated from our rational qualities, leading to a state of alienation from ourselves. Thus began our common experience of lonely individualism.

Descartes' philosophy led to a mechanical view of reality, which saw the universe as a kind of wind-up clock, whose springs, rods and cogs were set in motion by God, who remained separate from his creation. In the nineteenth century this mechanistic view was extended to people, who were also seen as machines, with their behaviour determined by laws corresponding to those of physics and chemistry. Spirit had been driven from the universe, leaving a cold, dark, empty and lonely space for us to make our home.

When this dualistic conception was extended to the Earth, our world lost all its value, its sacred quality and meaning, and became just dead matter, to be manipulated, exploited and degraded by science and technology in the name of human progress. Once the West lost its belief in God, it also lost belief in the sacredness of the soul, and succumbed to an almost wholly materialistic view of life, in which the highest value is given over to material things. This completely objective approach to life, with its denigration of any value in subjective experience, was the apotheosis of the masculine approach to life and nature.

This patriarchal and materialistic view of life dominated our thinking during the past three centuries. But in an odd act of reversal the Western mind, partly through new findings in science, is slowly finding its way to a conception of life and spirit that resembles Socrates' original ideas. The old deterministic and rigid view of existence has been replaced by a more open, free and creative view. Although we are now aware of the harm that the materialistic perspective causes, both individually and for society, this view of existence has penetrated so deeply into the human mind that it remains the foundation of our thinking, and shapes and conditions the way we see the world and talk about it. It will take a long time for it to be replaced with a different attitude towards reality – the ecological or systems view – a view that is similar to that expressed 2,400 years ago by Socrates.

The lessons of ecology, such as the Gaia theory, have taught us that the Earth is a living system and that we are embedded in a great web of life, in which our relationships within this web are the key to existence. We are not separate egos bouncing around in a world ruled by chance, but are part of an immensely large network of life and activity. Just as a tree cannot be separated from the Earth we cannot be separated from our total environment. We now see the world as a complicated tissue or net of events, in which connections of different kinds alternate or overlap or combine and thereby determine the texture of the whole. Instead of being isolated and lonely individuals, we are related intimately to all of creation.

What would the world be like now if the West had followed

Socrates' conception of the soul rather than Plato's? This is an impossible question to answer, but it is not impossible for us to use his soul model today, and it is clear that many people in the ecological movement and those who are trying to find a new living spirituality, have an integrated view of life similar to that held by Socrates. He can be seen as a trail-blazer for a new holistic and integrated view of life.

This is a view of reality that brings human consciousness and experience back into the centre of existence. Our knowledge that the universe is expanding, that evolution is an endless creative principle at the heart of life, are human conceptions and understandings, subjective reflections on our existence. We have realised we are the eyes and mind of the universe and that the 14 billion year history of the universe is, whether by chance, necessity or design, a movement that ultimately leads to human beings whose self-awareness gives the universe a self-reflective understanding of itself. Instead of seeing ourselves as insignificant creatures living a purposeless existence in a backwater of a vast universe that dwarves us, we are now able to tell a story of our existence that is creative and meaningful. This possibility of investing meaning into our lives, of understanding that the world is indeterminate and that our creative thought will play a significant role in any change that takes place on earth, gives us a future that may be full of danger but can also be full of hope. We can drop the arrogance of being masters of the universe and can once again become the children of the universe.

These first few years of our new century show that we need to develop all of our spiritual resources to cope with the challenges of fear, violence, aggression, terror and environmental degradation that it poses. Until we are able to make a mindshift away from the old paradigm that encourages competition, selfishness and greed, and learn to inhabit the new set of values that brings out co-operation and compassion, we will continue to commit the same mistakes that landed us in our present dilemma. We need to bring the distorted fragments of our separated souls into a healthy and restorative wholeness.

What is the importance of being whole, of being an integrated person, of establishing a unified view of existence? One of the most important reasons is that you can resolve the tension and conflicts between the inner world and the outside world. By seeing the world in oneness you understand that your inner being and its feelings and impulses and the outside world that you perceive are interrelated, so that one does not exist without the other. You understand that essentially they are the same thing.

The world that you perceive and the inner sense of who you are as an individual are not different realms of existence but are one unified realm. Life inside and life outside, nature and human nature, are one experience. You do not fall into the trap of dualism, with its attendant ills. Instead, you view the world outside with the same feelings that you have about yourself: trusting, positive, accepting, open and loving. In this way you project out from yourself feelings that encourage friendship and harmony in everyone you meet.

Although many people today have gone to Eastern religions and philosophies to find a spirituality like this, it seems clear to me that our own Western tradition began with a similar spirituality to that of the East. Unfortunately, this spirituality was buried under an excess of rationality, but now that people are turning again to a life infused with spirit, it is good to realise that at the source of our own tradition there was a person who managed to combine rationality and spirituality in a potent combination.

The finest praise I have seen for Socrates and his teaching is in a dialogue called *Theages*, which is probably not by Plato. In it, Theages, a former student, returns to Athens after many years to look for his old teacher, and has this to say:

I will tell you, Socrates, something incredible but true. I never at any time learnt anything from you, as you know. I made progress, however, when I associated with you, even if I was only in the same building, though not in the same room. But more so when I was in your presence, and I seemed to myself to improve much more when I looked at you when you were speaking, rather than when I looked away. But I made by far the greatest progress when I sat near you and touched you.

This is the teaching without words, the teaching that is transmitted from mind to mind, from soul to soul, and it is held in the East to be the best kind. Unfortunately, Socrates is no longer with us to transmit that personal teaching, but in an age when spirit and soul are once more making a comeback, his spirit lives on as an inspiration to all those who believe that life without meaning or purpose is not worth living. He reminds us that the knowledge of *aretē*, the excellence of the soul, is not only the highest form of knowledge that we can seek, but that it can lead us to new conceptions of goodness and beauty with which we can begin to heal ourselves and the world.

Mark Forstater
Queens Park, London, May 2003

Part Two

SOCRATES AND THE GENERAL

*Selections from Xenophon's
Memorabilia of Socrates*

A NOTE ON
THE TEXT

In making this selection of dialogues and conversations from Xenophon's *Memorabilia* I have used as my starting point J. S Watson's literal translation from 1871 which I have rewritten into contemporary English. I have taken quite a few liberties with the text, as scholars will no doubt appreciate (and some may not). In particular, I have imagined that Xenophon was either a witness or the actual subject of the dialogues that he reports, and I have placed him as a character in the dialogues to reflect this conjecture.

I have assumed that the relationship between the two men lasts for about nine years, from a time when Xenophon (428–354 BCE) is eighteen years old (410) to his departure for Persia in 401 when he is twenty-seven.

Chapters 1 and 11 are based on anecdotes from Diogenes Laertius. Chapter 2 is originally a dialogue with Euthydemus the handsome, whom I have replaced in the dialogue with Xenophon. The stories of Chapters 3,4,5 and 6 did not originally include Xenophon, whom I have added, and Chapter 7 was a conversation with an unnamed young man, whom I have replaced with Xenophon. In Chapter 4, I have also taken the liberty of having Socrates give Xenophon an affectionate nickname, 'General', that is not in the original. Finally, I have taken a portion of Plato's dialogue *Euthydemus*, and used it as the basis for Chapter 9, since its theme of happiness and wisdom seems to fit with Xenophon's learning curve.

My reason for making these alterations is to create a more integral and flowing narrative and to make the material more attractive both for me to write and hopefully for readers to read. There is no scholarly justification for making these changes, only authorial ones.

1

THE MEETING

*In Which the Young Xenophon
Meets the Old Philosopher*

It was one of those golden late afternoons in spring that you often get in Athens. The sun bathed the stones as the day slowed down. I was eighteen, a strong, handsome young man walking quickly home from the gymnasium. As I went up a narrow passageway near the marketplace, an old man stretched a stick in front of me and barred my way.

I stopped in surprise and looked up at him. I must have been shocked, because I didn't say anything, but just stared at him, because his face and body gave out two contradictory and striking images.

First, he was ugly – pug ugly. He had a wide, upturned nose with huge nostrils; his face was broad and his eyes popped out, so that he looked exactly like the God Pan. He had long hair and a great bushy beard, neither of which looked at all clean. We Greeks love beauty, both natural and man-made, and ugliness of this magnitude is positively upsetting to us. How could Nature have made this man so repellent?

But underneath his simple cloak I could see that his body was quite imposing. He may have been in his late fifties but he was quite fit and held himself upright with some bearing. He looked like someone who could take care of himself in a fight if he needed to. He was barefoot and his feet were broad, with splayed-out toes.

This combination of ugliness and strength made a strong impression. Looking into his face I could see a sly, impudent look, and his eyes sparkled with liveliness and intelligence. He peered closely at me and spoke very seriously,

'Do you know where I can find some full-bodied wine?'

The question surprised me, but I recommended a wine merchant my father always used.

'And where I can get some ripe olives?'

Again I told him of a seller I knew in the market.

'And how about finding a beautiful tunic like yours?'

I was puzzled about where these questions were leading? Did I look like an Athenian shopping guide?

He then said, pointedly, 'And where can I find someone who knows about how people become good and who moulds excellent character?'

'There I can't help you,' I said, starting to push past his outstretched stick.

He put a hand out to restrain me. 'But there I may be able to help you,' he said. I stopped and looked at him again. He wasn't joking.

'My name is Socrates. Follow me and learn, if you are interested.'

As we walked together I told him my name and about my family. He explained that every day he could be found either in the marketplace, or at one of the city's gymnasia, talking to people of all kinds, but especially to his friends, about many subjects, but his main concern was with excellence, justice and goodness and how to acquire them. If I was interested in learning I should join him, since his friends all seemed to value these discussions.

2

A FIRST LESSON

*In Which Xenophon
Learns about his Limitations*

One morning Socrates surprised me by coming into a saddlemaker's shop, where I was on business. Was he just passing by, or had he deliberately sought me out?

He looked genuinely surprised to see me, and called out, 'Xenophon, what are you doing here?'

'My father is giving me a new saddle, so I wanted to see what I can afford.'

'Do you like to ride?'

'I've been riding all my life; it's one of my great pleasures.'

He sat down on a stool and gestured for me to join him. 'I was wondering, Xenophon, what you were interested in doing with your life? I mean, do you have an ambition to learn something specific?'

I thought hard before making a reply, since I wasn't sure how Socrates would respond to my ambition, which I had never revealed to anyone.

Since my silence lasted a little too long, he continued, 'For example, do you want to become skilled in managing government, to become qualified to benefit yourself and everyone else?'

'Socrates, what I would really like is the ability to command an army, to be a general.'

'Well, that's an honourable but difficult accomplishment, Xenophon. Have you ever considered whether it's possible for someone who is not a just person to become a great commander?'

'I have, and I think that it's not possible to be even a good citizen without a sense of justice.'

'And have you made yourself a master of that virtue?'

'I think, Socrates, that I am no less just than any other person.'

'Really? Good. Then, let me ask you this. Do there exist works of just people, in the same way as there exist works of artists?'

'I'm sure there must be.'

'So, just as artists are able to show their work, wouldn't just people be able to talk about theirs?'

'I think it's very possible to talk about the works of justice, and of injustice, for I see and hear them every day.'

He paused for a second and then nodded. 'Would you like to talk about them now?'

'What, here?' I wasn't sure a saddlemaker's shop was the right place to discuss justice, but he dismissed my objection. 'Justice and injustice are found everywhere, Xenophon, so why not here and now?'

If it didn't bother him, why should I object, so I agreed.

He began, 'Look, I'll draw a vertical line on the ground , and write *justice* on one side, and *injustice* on the other, and we'll put whatever seems to us to be a work of justice or a work of injustice under the correct heading.'

'That sounds fine,' I said, a little nervously. What had I let myself in for?

Socrates then drew the words in the sand, and put a line between them.

Justice	Injustice

Then he looked at me and asked, 'Does lying exist among mankind?'

That was easy. 'Indeed it does.'

'Under which heading should we put lying?'

'Under injustice, certainly,' I said.

He wrote it down. 'Does deceit also exist?'

'Of course,' I replied.

'And under what heading?'

'Injustice again,' I said.

He wrote that down. 'And does piracy exist?'

'Yes.'

'And slavery?'

'Yes.'

'And should we place either of these under justice, Xenophon?'

'Not at all,' I said.

Socrates wrote them down, and when he finished we both looked at the drawing:

Justice	Injustice
	lying
	deceit
	piracy
	slavery

He looked over at me, and said, 'So all of these things: lying, deceit, piracy and slavery are all unjust acts?'

'That's right,' I agreed. This wasn't so bad. I began to relax a little.

He continued to look at me, but a little more intently. 'So if the commander of an army should make slaves of an unjust and hostile population, we would have to say that he committed an act of injustice.'

I hesitated. 'I don't think we can.'

'Do you think we should say instead that he acted justly?'

This was getting a little tricky. 'I would have to say so.' But even as I said it, I wondered in my own mind if that could really be correct?

Socrates continued, 'And if in the course of this war, he has to practise deceit?'

'I suppose that would also have to be just.'

'So if he steals and carries off their property, would he not be doing a just thing?'

I started to get flustered and blurted out, 'Certainly it's just against our enemies, but I thought you were asking questions only about our allies.'

'I understand. But do you still agree that everything that we originally placed under the heading of injustice: lying, deceit, piracy, and slavery, we are now obliged to place under the heading of justice?'

'It looks like it,' I quietly admitted.

He now wrote them down under justice, so that the drawing in the sand looked like this:

Justice	Injustice
lying	lying
deceit	deceit
piracy	piracy
slavery	slavery

We both looked at the drawing, and he turned to me, with a slightly amused look on his face.

'Interesting, isn't it? We now see that the idea of justice is not so simple or easy.'

'No, it's certainly more complicated than I thought.'

'Xenophon, perhaps it would be best if we made a new distinction: that it is just to do these things with regard to our enemies, but unjust to do them to our friends, and that towards his friends our general should be as open and straight-forward as possible?'

'I think so,' I said.

'But then,' said Socrates, 'what if our general notices that his army is suffering from low morale, and he tells them, by inventing a lie, that reinforcements are coming, and by this lie he stops their dejection, under which heading would we place such an act of deceit: just or unjust?'

'I would have to place it under the heading of justice.'

'And if a parent, when his child requires medicine, and refuses to take it, should deceive him, and give him the medicine as ordinary food, and by adopting such a deception, restore him to health, under which heading should we place this act of deceit?'

'This also should go under the same heading.'

'And if a person, finding his friend badly depressed, should, through fear that he might kill himself, steal his sword, under what heading should we place that act?'

'That, too, under the heading of justice.'

'So really, Xenophon, you're saying that even towards our friends we cannot always act without deceit?'

'It looks like I am, Socrates, and I need to retract what I said before, if I can do that.'

'It's better that you do, rather than place actions on the wrong side. But just so that we don't leave any point unexamined, of those who deceive their friends in order to injure them, which of the two is the more unjust, the person who does so deliberately or the person who does so involuntarily?'

On hearing this question, my face must have turned a shade of grey, and I said, 'Socrates, I am not at all confident that I can give you answers to your questions; for everything I have said so far contradicts everything I thought I believed.'

'Don't get upset, Xenophon, but just try to answer as you really believe.'

'Well, then, let me say that the person who deceives intentionally is more unjust than the person who deceives unintentionally.'

'Xenophon, do you think there is a way to learn and know what is just, as there is of learning and knowing how to read and write?'

'I think there is.'

'And is the better student the one who reads and writes incorrectly on purpose or the one who does it through ignorance?'

'It must be the one who does it purposefully, for whenever he wants to, he could also do it correctly.'

'So the one who on purpose writes incorrectly may in fact be a good student, but the person who reads badly involuntarily is lacking scholarship?'

'How can it be otherwise?'

'Then does that mean that the person who lies and deceives intentionally really knows what is just, or is it the person who lies unawares who knows justice?'

'Doubtless, the one who does it intentionally.'

'You therefore say that the person who can read and write is a better student than the person who is ignorant?'

'Of course.'

'And that the person who knows what is just is more just than the person who does not know?'

My speech now became much slower, as if the words were somehow being dragged out of me. I can't explain what came over me, but it was as if words were somehow coming into my brain through a narrow sieve. 'I . . . seem . . . to be saying this. But how I come to be saying it I must admit I do not know.'

'But you do admit it? That the person who knows what justice is, is a more just person than the one who is ignorant of justice?'

'I do believe that is true.'

'Then tell me, Xenophon, what would you think of someone who, wanting to tell the truth, would never give the same account of the same thing, but, for example, in speaking of the same road, would say at one time that it led towards the east and another time towards the west, or in stating the result of a maths calculation, would sometimes assert the answer to be twenty, and sometimes to be fifteen. What would you think of such a person?'

'It would be quite obvious that he knew nothing of what he claimed to know.'

'Good. Then let us look at our drawing again.'

I didn't need to look, because it slowly dawned on me that the person I had just described as knowing nothing of what he claimed to know, was . . . *me*! I had also tried to tell the truth as I saw it, but every time I gave an answer it was different. I was completely ignorant and he could see it so clearly.

I glanced over at him in my embarrassment, and he was looking at me with a patient and kindly face.

'Xenophon, do you know any people who can be called slave-like?'

'I do.'

'Do we call them this because of their knowledge or their ignorance?'

'For their ignorance.'

'Is it for their ignorance in metalwork that we call them slave-like?'

'Not at all.'

'Or for their ignorance of shoemaking, or building?'

'No.'

'Is it that the name "slave-like" is applied to those who are ignorant of what is honourable, just and good?'

'I think so.'

'We therefore need to exert ourselves as much as possible to avoid acting like ignorant slaves, especially if our ambition is to command armies.'

I didn't know what to say. I had always thought that I was a person striving after excellence, virtue and honour, and knew what that meant. But now I felt completely dispirited when I realised that I was unable to answer a simple question about what I needed most of all to know. I was totally lost and had no idea how to remedy it or how to become better.

Socrates must have sensed how I was feeling, because he changed the subject,

'Tell me, Xenophon, have you ever gone to Delphi, to consult the oracle there?'

'Twice,' I said.

'And did you notice what is written there on the temple wall: KNOW YOURSELF.'

'I did.'

'Did you give any thought to that inscription, to try to examine yourself, so that you could understand what sort of character you have?'

'I didn't try, since I thought at the time that I knew myself pretty well. I could hardly know anything else if I didn't know myself.'

'But can you truly know yourself if all you know is your name or what you like to eat or the job you would like to do?'

'Those are only surface facts, not real knowledge.'

'Then let's compare you to people who buy horses. They don't think they know the horse until they have determined if it is obedient or unruly, or strong or weak, swift or slow, and all the other points in which a horse can be useful or disadvantaged. In the same way, shouldn't a person determine with regard to himself how he is adapted to the service of mankind, and to know his own abilities?'

'I agree that someone who doesn't know his own abilities doesn't know himself.'

'And Xenophon, isn't it also evident that people enjoy a great number of blessings because they know themselves, and incur a great number of evils because they are deluded about themselves?'

'How is that, Socrates?'

'Because the people who really know themselves know what is suitable for them, and can distinguish between what they can and cannot do. By doing what they know how to do, they succeed in life, and are prosperous, and by abstaining from what they do not know, they live blameless lives and avoid misfortune.

'Through having this deep knowledge of themselves, they are able to form an accurate opinion of others, and through their experience of dealing with the rest of mankind, they obtain for themselves what is good, and they guard themselves against what is evil.

'People who have not bothered to really know themselves, but are deluded about their own powers and abilities, find themselves in exactly the same state with other people and experiences, which they also cannot understand or have real knowledge of.

'They neither understand what their own characters need or what they are actually doing, and they fail to judge the characters of those with whom they are dealing, and being in error in all these cases, they fail to obtain what is good and instead fall into evil.

'But the people who understand what they take in hand normally succeed in what they attempt, and become esteemed and honoured. Others who resemble them in character willingly make connections with them. Meanwhile, those who are unsuccessful in life want other people to deliberate or assist them with their advice, and prefer others to themselves. They place in them their hopes for good, and love them, on all these accounts, beyond all other people.

'And again, those who do not know what they are doing, who make an unhappy choice in life, and are unsuccessful in what they attempt, not only incur losses and suffering on their own account, but become in consequence, disreputable and ridiculous, and drag out their lives in contempt and dishonour.

'Among states, too, you see some that, from ignorance of their own strength, go to war with others that are more powerful and become utterly overthrown, and still others are reduced from freedom to slavery.

'Do you understand what I am getting at, Xenophon?'

'I understand that a deep self-knowledge is essential. But as to how to seek it, I have no idea.'

'Perhaps you haven't given enough thought to all these matters, from a belief that you were already well acquainted with them.'

'My own lack of insight, Socrates, obliges me to admit that this is so. I am wondering whether it would be best for me to remain silent, for it seems to me that I actually know nothing.'

I left the shop in great dejection and despair, holding myself in contempt, and thinking that in reality I was no better than the most ignorant of the ignorant.

I realised that I could find no better way to improve my character than by listening to Socrates as much as possible. In consequence, for a period of time I never left his side unless some urgent business took me away. I also began to imitate a number of Socrates' habits of living.

When Socrates noticed that I was acting like this, he no longer puzzled me with questions, but explained to me, in the simplest and clearest manner, what he thought that I ought to know, and what it would be best for me to study.

And so I became what we called a follower or a friend or an associate of Socrates. We were not students since he claimed not to teach us anything, but we just discussed things that he found of interest. Although he claimed to know nothing, his knowledge of a vast range of subjects never ceased to amaze me.

3

GOOD LEARNING

*In Which Xenophon
Becomes 'Dignified'*

Early one morning I joined Socrates for a workout at the Academy, one of his favourite gymnasia. After bathing, I went to get us some cool drinking water, and when I sat down beside him, and gave him his cup, he turned to me with a quizzical look.

'Have you ever heard of a man called Dionysodorus?'

'No,' I said, 'Where's he from?'

'He's Boeotian, and he's just returned from Thracia where he says he was commander of a large body of troops.'

Socrates knew that my dream was to become a military commander, although as yet I hadn't done anything about it, except talk.

'Do you believe him?' I asked.

'Well, he looks the part, anyway; he's got the scars to prove it. He's set up shop as a teacher of the Art of War.'

'Really. Do you think I should look him up?'

'Well, Xenophon, if you really do want to become a commander then you shouldn't neglect any opportunity to learn. During a war the entire state is under the care of a general, and if he's skilful, great advantages accrue to the state. But if he fails, then the evils are immense. Since

Dionysodorus claims to know about these skills, maybe you should go and study with him.'

So I located Dionysodorus and for a period of time became his student. It cost me quite a lot of money, but I felt it was worthwhile to begin to make progress towards my goal.

Later, I returned to Socrates' circle, and he began to joke with me in front of the others,

'Homer, in the *Iliad*, styles the warrior Agamemnon as "dignified". Now, doesn't our Xenophon, after learning how to be a general, seem to you to look more dignified than before?'

Everyone agreed, pulling dignified faces at me, and taking military poses. I felt distinctly uncomfortable.

Socrates could see that he had an appreciative audience, so he carried on.

'Just as we say that someone who learns to play the lyre is a lyrist, though he may not use the instrument, and one who learns the art of healing is a physician, even if he does not practice medicine, so this young man will from now on be a general, though he may never be given a command.

'So I propose that from this time on we all address our friend not as Xenophon but as "The General".'

Everyone had a good laugh, and I felt like a fool, but when I looked over at Socrates I saw that although he was mocking me he wasn't being malicious, but had an affectionate look on his face. I'll never forget that look, because I could see that he really approved of what I was doing, and his approval meant more to me than anything else. And from that day onwards, true to his word, Socrates never failed to call me 'The General', and took the trouble to discuss with me subjects that related to leadership qualities.

But he wasn't finished tormenting me yet. His face turned more serious and he said, 'General, in future some of us may have to command a troop under you. I think we will need some knowledge of the art of war. Can you tell us how Dionysodorus began to teach you generalship?'

I had no choice, I had to answer. 'He began,' I said, 'with the same thing with which he ended, which was tactics.'

Socrates looked surprised.

'Only tactics? Nothing else?'

'That's right.'

'But tactics are only a small part of the qualifications of a general! For a general has to be skilful in preparing everything that is necessary for war. He must be able to secure provisions for his troops, and be a man of great contrivance and activity, careful, persevering and sagacious; kind to his men, yet severe; open, yet crafty; careful of his own, yet ready to steal from others; profuse, yet rapacious; lavish of presents, yet eager to acquire money; cautious, yet enterprising; and many other qualities which a general of ability must possess.'

I thought it was right to try to defend my new teacher, 'Dionysodorus says that if a general isn't skilled in tactics then he can't plan a battle.'

'Of course,' said Socrates, 'that's an important skill; because a well-arranged army is very different from a disorderly one. I would compare it to building a house: if the stones, bricks, wood and tiles are thrown together in a pile, they are useless; but when the stones and tiles, which are the materials not likely to rot or decay, are placed at the bottom and the top, and the bricks and wood are arranged in the middle, then a valuable property can be formed.'

Now it was my turn to be surprised. 'What you've said is an exact illustration of Dionysodorus' teaching; because in battle we place the bravest troops in the front and rear, and the more cowardly in the middle, so that the cowardly are led on by those braver than themselves, and pushed forward by those behind.'

Socrates nodded in approval. 'That rule sounds excellent, as long as your teacher taught you how to tell the difference between the brave and the cowardly. Did he?'

'No,' I said sheepishly.

'Well then, what benefit is there, General, in what you've learned? For example, if he asked you, in arranging a number of coins, to lay the good ones first and last, and the worst ones in the middle, and gave you no instruction in how to tell the good ones from the duds, his orders to you would be completely useless.'

My heart sinking, I realised that my training had not been very thorough, and that Socrates seemed to have more knowledge of the art of war than the so-called expert. It looked like I had wasted my money.

I replied, 'Since he didn't teach me how to tell the brave from the cowardly, I suppose this is something I need to find out for myself.'

'Would you like us to consider how to do it?'

'Of course.'

'All right – now, if we wanted to try to obtain some money, and were to place the greediest man in front, do you think we would have arranged our men properly?'

'I think so.'

'Good. So what do generals do when they are entering on a dangerous enterprise? Shouldn't they place the most ambitious soldiers in front? These are the ones who are ready to brave danger for the sake of praise; and they are not difficult to discover, because they make themselves conspicuous and are easy to select.

'Now, did your instructor teach you to arrange an army, only, or did he tell you for what purpose, and in what manner, you must employ each division of your forces?'

'I'm afraid he gave us no instructions about this.'

Socrates considered this. He then said, 'If I were you, General, I would go back to *Commander* Dionysodorus, and ask him about this; for if he knows, and is not completely shameless, he'll feel guilty about taking your money, and sending you away in complete ignorance.'

The next day I returned to Dionysodorus and told him what Socrates had said. He was furious that Socrates had questioned his teaching, and called him a mangy, fraudulent Sophist. But after cooling down, he agreed to give me a few more lessons at no further cost. I felt that I was finally on the road to becoming a commander.

But where, I wondered, had Socrates received all this knowledge about war and military matters?

4

VIRTUE AND VICE

Socrates Admonishes his Former Pupil Aristippus

Aristippus had moved from Cyrene to Athens because of the fame of Socrates, and he became one of his most devoted students. But Aristippus came to believe that he should seek only the pleasure of the moment and not worry at all about future pleasures or other considerations. He did not want to abstain from pleasures but instead to indulge them, as long as he could keep control and not be overcome by them.

He once said, on entering a brothel, 'Going in is not dangerous, it is being unable to come out that is the problem.' What he wanted was not abstinence from pleasures, but mastery over them, without being overcome by them. This is a difficult path to travel, since we know that pleasure, especially sensual pleasure, has a tremendous force, like wild horses, and to stop them once they have started takes a mind and will of great power.

Aristippus decided that there were only two states of feeling: pleasure and pain. He said that pleasure is never differentiated and is always the same, no matter where it is found, and it is attractive to all creatures. He believed pleasure was the ultimate good, and that everything else was a means to it.

Aristippus believed that when we were in pleasure we

needed nothing else. Bodily pleasure was greater than mental pleasure, and bodily pain the worst of all. Consequently, Aristippus and the school he founded paid more attention to the body than to the mind.

For Aristippus a truly pleasurable life was one of pleasure following pleasure, with no let-up. Socrates said that this was like constantly needing to replenish a leaking jar, and was both tedious and unsustainable.

One day Socrates asked me if I had heard about Aristippus' new house. I told him that everyone was talking about how luxurious it was, and how Aristippus was spending a fortune on feasts and parties. Socrates said that Aristippus had asked him over for a drink and he wondered if I would like to tag along. Given an opportunity to hear two philosophers speak was not something I wanted to turn down.

When we arrived at the house, a slave let us in, and we were both struck by the magnificence of the silks and brocades covering the chairs and couches. The walls were painted with colourful and glorious images from Homer and the poets. We both looked around the room with our mouths open.

The slave interrupted our reverie by offering us a seat and a glass of wine and water, when Aristippus grandly swept in to greet us.

'Socrates – and Xenophon, what a surprise! Welcome to my humble abode!'

'I hardly call this humble, Aristippus, where did you get so much?'

Aristippus replied, 'Where you got so little, Socrates.'

'I heard you've set up as a teacher, and are charging money for it as well.'

'Not just money, Socrates, but extremely large fees. Just this morning a man brought his son to me and asked me to teach him. I agreed, of course, and said it would cost five hundred drachmas.'

Socrates nearly choked on his wine when he heard this sum. Aristippus continued, 'The father reacted just like you, and he said, "For that much money I can buy a slave!" Then do so, I said, and the consequence will be that you will have two slaves in your household.'

Aristippus laughed loudly at his own joke, and reached for his cup of wine. Socrates was not quite so amused.

'So, did the father decline your kind offer?'

'Not at all. In fact, he left me a very hefty deposit.'

And with that comment, he reached over to a nearby table, pulled out a drawer and took out a beautiful blue silken purse which he picked up between his fingers. Moving the purse in Socrates' direction, he offered it to him.

'Go on, take it, I owe you so much!'

Socrates looked annoyed, the first time I ever saw him so disturbed. Normally he was always in good humour.

'If I taught you anything, Aristippus, it must have been unintentional, since as you know I have nothing to teach. I never charged you for listening to me, so there is no need to make the offer. I'm grateful you appreciate me, but I can't accept.'

'Don't be such a hypocrite, Socrates. Of course I take fees, and so do you, because your rich friends send you gifts of corn, food, oil and wine, of which you take what you need and return the rest. You have the most prominent men of Athens as your stewards, whereas I must do with my slave.'

Socrates turned red. 'They voluntarily offer me these things, Aristippus, as friends do, and not because I demand it or as an exchange for services rendered.'

Socrates nodded at the blue purse which still dangled in front of him. 'This money is gained from prostituting knowledge and I can't accept it from you. I also don't need it. My needs are simple, unlike yours.'

Aristippus looked peeved as he swung the bag out of Socrates' way and replaced it in the drawer. He explained, 'I only wanted to repay you for all the wonderful discussions and teaching you gave me.'

Socrates had calmed down by now and gone back to his

normal self. He said, 'From what I can see, and what I hear about your latest ideas, I don't think I taught you anything. In fact, I would be ashamed to be called your teacher.'

Aristippus looked hurt and deflated. There was an uncomfortable silence which Socrates broke, 'Aristippus, let me ask you something.'

'Ask away, Socrates.'

'Let's say you were given the job of educating two young people, one in such a way that he would be qualified to govern the state, and the other in such a way that he would have no desire to govern, how would you go about training them? Can you start with first principles, by discussing say, their food?'

'Food is certainly important,' replied Aristippus, 'since a person can't live without eating.'

'Would it be natural for them,' asked Socrates, 'to be hungry at specific times?'

'I think so,' said Aristippus.

'And which of the two,' asked Socrates, 'would you train to prefer to finish any urgent business before satisfying his hunger?'

'The one,' replied Aristippus, 'who is being prepared to rule, since the affairs of state must not be neglected.'

'And when they are thirsty, should we, of the same person, insist on the ability to endure thirst?'

'Absolutely,' replied Aristippus.

'And which of the two should we require to be moderate in sleep, so as to be able to go to bed late, to rise early, or to remain awake if needed?'

'Of the same one, no doubt.'

'And which of the two would we expect to control sensual appetites, so that he is not disturbed by their influence from performing whatever duty he faces?'

'Again the same one.'

'And which of the two would you encourage not to shrink from work, but willingly to go for it.'

'The same.'

'And to which of the two would it be best to provide knowledge that would assist in giving authority over any rivals?'

'Far more to the one who is trained to govern, for without knowledge there would be no benefit in any of the other qualifications.'

'If you trained this person in such a way, do you think he would be less likely to be surprised by his enemies than other animals are?'

'How do you mean?'

'Well, we know that some animals are captured by their need for food, and others, though very shy, are still attracted to bait by their desire to eat, and are consequently caught; while others are trapped by drink.'

'Our young trainee would not be trapped like that,' said Aristippus.

'And aren't there other animals captured by their sexual needs, like quails and partridges, which, being attracted to the call of the female by desire and the hope of pleasure, and lose all sense of danger and fall into traps?'

Aristippus again agreed.

'And since many essential occupations of life, such as those of war, agriculture and others are carried on in the open air, doesn't it appear to you to show great negligence, that the majority of mankind should be wholly untrained to endure heat and cold?'

Aristippus agreed.

'Doesn't it then appear to you that we should train our potential ruler to bear these things without difficulty?'

'Of course,' replied Aristippus.

'If, therefore, we class those able to endure these things among those who are qualified to govern, shall we not class those who are unable to endure them among those who will not even aspire to govern?'

'Definitely,' he said.

'Since you know the position of each of these classes of

people, I wonder if you have ever considered in which one you would place yourself?'

'Of course I have,' said Aristippus, 'and I certainly don't place myself in the class of those desiring to rule. It seems to me that, when it is difficult enough to even obtain the things necessary to sustain one's own self, it is the mark of a very foolish man to not be satisfied with just that task, but to add to it the difficulty of procuring the very same things for his fellow countrymen.

'I consider it the greatest stupidity, that while many things he desires are out of his reach, he should, by setting himself at the head of the state, subject himself, if he does not accomplish everything that the people want, to be criticized for his failure.

'For the people think it their right to use their rulers as I use my slaves. I expect my slaves to supply me with the necessaries of life in abundance, but to take no part of them for themselves. And the people think it the duty of their rulers to supply them with as many benefits as possible, but for they themselves to abstain from having any of them.

'Those, therefore, who wish to undergo a great deal of effort and trouble for themselves, and to also give trouble to others, I would train in this manner, and consider them qualified to govern. But myself I number with those who wish to pass their lives in the greatest possible ease and pleasure.'

Socrates then said, 'Will you allow us to consider this point also, whether the rulers or the ruled live with the greater pleasure?'

'By all means,' said Aristippus.

'In the first place then, of the nations we know of, the Persians are rulers in Asia, and the Syrians, Phrygians and Lydians are under their subjection. The Scythians govern in Europe, and the Maeotians are held in subjection. The Carthaginians rule in North Africa, and the Libyans are under their power. There is no question which of these is living under the greater pleasure is there? Or among the Greeks, of whom you are one, which of the two appear to you to live more happily, those who rule or those who are in subjection?'

'Socrates, I don't consider myself to be living in subjection. There appears to me to be a middle path between the two, in which I try to travel, and which leads not through slavery, but through liberty, a path that most surely leads to happiness.'

'If this path of yours,' said Socrates, 'which lies neither through sovereignty nor servitude, did not also lie through human society, what you say would be worth considering. But if, while living among mankind, you do not think it proper to rule or to be ruled, and you are not willing to pay respect to those in power, I think that you will see that the strong know very well how to treat the weak as slaves, making them complain both publicly and privately.

'Surely you know about gangs who attack and destroy the crops and orchards of those who have sown and planted them. These people abuse and intimidate those who are weaker than themselves, as well as those who are unwilling to flatter and pay court to them, until they prevail on the weak to prefer slavery to carrying on a war against their superior power? In private life, too, don't you see that the spirited and strong enslave the timid and weak, and enjoy the fruits of their work?'

Aristippus replied, 'This is true, and to avoid suffering like them, I am not going to restrict myself to any one place, but shall become a citizen of the world.'

'No doubt,' replied Socrates, 'this is an excellent idea; for ever since Theseus killed the great robbers, everyone knows the highways are completely safe. But consider how those who govern in the various countries pass laws so that they cannot be injured, and ally to themselves, in addition to their relatives and friends, many other supporters. See how they surround their cities with ramparts and walls, buy weapons to repel aggressors, and secure other allies from abroad. Yet even these rulers who have provided themselves with all these defences still suffer injury. And do you, having no protection of this kind, spending a long time on dangerous roads on which many travellers are injured, weaker than all the inhabitants of whatever city you arrive at, and being the kind of target those who are eager to commit violence most readily attack, think, nevertheless, that you will not be wronged because you are a stranger?

'Do you think that if you were kidnapped and sold into slavery that you would be such a poor slave that you would profit no master. For who would wish to keep in his house a man who is not interested in working, and yet delights in the most expensive diet?

'Let's consider how slave-owners treat slaves like this? Don't they tame their fondness for delicacies by hunger? Don't they stop them from stealing by excluding them from every place where there is anything to take? Don't they stop them from running away by putting them in chains? Don't they overcome their laziness with a whip?

'How do you act, Aristippus, when you find one of your slaves in this kind of disposition?'

'I chastise him,' said Aristippus, 'with every kind of punishment, until I compel him to serve me. But Socrates, how do those who are trained for the art of ruling, which it seems to me you consider as happiness, differ from those who undergo hardships from necessity, since they will also have (though it is by their own consent) to endure hunger, thirst, cold, heat, lack of sleep and other difficulties?

'For I don't see what difference it makes to a man who is whipped, if the whipping is voluntary or involuntary. In short, to the one who suffers, does it matter if he suffers with or without his consent? I certainly think that folly is to be attributed to one who endures troubles voluntarily.'

Socrates replied, 'Don't voluntary sufferings of this kind seem to you to differ from involuntary, since the person who is hungry from choice may eat when he pleases, while the one who endures hunger from necessity cannot relieve that hunger when he wishes? Besides, one who undergoes troubles willingly is sustained in undergoing it with some expectation of good, just as hunters willingly bear fatigue in the hope of capturing wild animals.

'And such rewards of effort are of small worth. But for those who exert themselves so that they can acquire valuable friends, or that they may subdue their enemies, or they may, by becoming strong in mind and body, manage their own household competently, and be of service to their friends and of advantage to their country, how can you think that they work for such purposes otherwise than cheerfully, or that they do not live in happiness, esteeming themselves, and being praised and envied by others?

'For neither laziness nor pleasures are capable of producing a well-constituted body, as the gym teachers say, nor do they bring to the mind any knowledge worthy of consideration. But exercises pursued with a persistent effort lead people to the attainment of good and valuable ends, as worthy people inform us; the poet Hesiod somewhere says:

Vice is possible to find in abundance and with ease; for the way to it is smooth and lies very near. But before the Temple of Virtue the immortal gods have placed effort, and the way to it is long and steep, and the beginning is rough; but when the traveller has arrived at the summit, it then becomes easy, however difficult it was at first.

A thought to which Epicharmus gives his testimony:

The gods for toil sell us all good things.

And in another place he says:

O wretched mortal, desire not what is easy, lest you find what is difficult.

Let me tell you a story that Prodicus the Sophist used to tell about Hercules, which he would declaim to anyone as an example of his story-telling ability. This story expresses a similar notion respecting virtue:

Hercules, when he was growing from boyhood to manhood, a period in which the young, becoming more mature, begin to show whether they will enter life by the path of virtue or that of vice, went out into the wilderness, and there sat down, confused as to which of these two paths he should choose.

He saw in the distance two giant female figures advancing towards him, one of them dressed all in white, and adorned with an engaging and graceful manner of walking. She was gifted by nature with a slim elegance, a downward look of solemn modesty, and a calm serenity to her gestures.

The second woman wore a see-through gown and had her face made up to look white and rosy, almost like a mask. She was plump and soft, and her gaze was bold. She glanced from side to side to see if anyone was observing her, and she frequently looked back at her own shadow.

As they approached closer to Hercules, the elegant woman maintained the same pace, but the second one, bolder and more eager to get to him, ran right up to Hercules and said:

'I see that you are perplexed, Hercules, in choosing which path to take to enter life; if you will be my friend, I can show you the easiest and most delightful road, on which you can taste every kind of pleasure, and lead a life free from all trouble.

'You shall have no thought of affairs of state, but shall spend your days wondering what kind of rare foods and drink you can find to gratify your appetite, what beautiful objects you can discover to delight your eyes, what harmonious sounds to lull your ears, what sweet odours to smell and what smooth and luxurious objects to stroke. And you will seek many other delightful objects of affection to give you the maximum pleasure that can be found, and at the end of your day you may sleep most softly and dream only pleasant dreams. All of these enjoyments can be found with the least amount of trouble.

'And if you ever feel any anxiety that you will not be able to afford these delights, don't worry that I will force you to obtain them by work, or by any suffering of body or mind; but you will be able to enjoy what others have worked for, and you will not restrain yourself from any kind of activity from which it may be possible to find profit, for I give my followers license to seize whatever they want from any source whatsoever.'

Hercules, on hearing this speech, said, 'And what, oh beautiful one, is your name?'

'My friends,' she said, 'call me Happiness, but those who dislike me disparage me by giving me the name of Vice.'

By this time the second woman had arrived, and she spoke. 'I have also come to speak with you, Hercules, because I know your parents, and I observed how they raised you during your childhood, from which I have hopes that if you follow the path that leads to my house, you will become an excellent example of whatever is good and meritorious, and through your actions I shall be seen as more valuable and attractive.

'But I will not deceive you with promises of pleasure, but must tell you how things really are in this world, and how the gods have set things up.

'For everything that is valuable and excellent, the gods will not give to mankind without some effort and care; so if you want the gods to be favourable to you, you must worship them; if you want to be loved by your friends, you must try to serve them and look after their interests; if you desire to be honoured by your city or country, you must benefit them with some advantage; if you feel anxious about the earth yielding you an abundance of fruits for your sustenance, you must cultivate the earth; if you want to enrich yourself with cattle, you must bestow care on those animals; if you are eager to secure freedom for your friends and subdue your enemies, you must learn the arts of war; if you wish to be vigorous in body, you must train your body to obey your mind, and exercise it with effort.'

Here Vice, interrupting her speech, said:

'Do you see, Hercules, how difficult and tedious a road this woman wants you to follow, while I can lead you, by an easy and short path, to perfect happiness.'

The graceful woman countered:

'Wretched woman, what good is it to possess you? What real pleasure do you experience, when you aren't willing to do anything to attain it? You, who don't even wait for the natural desire of gratification, but gorge yourself with all sorts of delicacies before you have an appetite for them, eating before you are hungry, drinking before you are thirsty, procuring cooks to save you effort, buying costly wines to drink with pleasure, and looking for everything rare and difficult to obtain.

'In order to sleep you not only have the softest beds, but have them fitted like suspended rocking cradles. And you need this because you don't sleep from exhaustion, but from the effort of doing nothing at all; you force sensual inclinations before they need gratification, using every kind of contrivance for the purpose, and abusing male and female; for this is how you treat your friends, insulting their modesty at night, and making them sleep away the most useful part of the day.

'Though you are one of the Immortals, you have been cast out from the society of the gods, and are despised by good people; the sweetest of all sounds – praise – you have never heard, nor have you seen the most pleasing of all sights, for you have never beheld even one excellent work of your own hands. Would anyone believe you if you gave your word? Would anyone assist you if you were in need? Or who, that has genuine feelings, would venture to join your band of revellers? For when they are young, they grow weaker in body, and when they are older, they become weak in the mind; when young, they live off the fat of the land, and have to endure suffering and anguish when old; remorseful at what they have done, oppressed with what they now must do to survive,

*having run through their pleasures in their youth, and oppressed
with illness at the close of life.*

*'But my name is Virtue, and I am the companion of the
gods; I associate only with real people; no good deed, human
or divine, is done without my help; I am respected, most of
all, by the deities, and by those on Earth who try to follow me,
since I co-operate with people who work with their hands and
minds, am a faithful guardian to those who run households, a
helpful assistant to servants, a benign promoter of peace, and
an excellent sharer in friendship.*

*'My friends have a simple and untroubled enjoyment of food
and drink, for they eat only when they are hungry and drink
only when they are thirsty; they sleep only when tired, and their
sleep is sweet; they are not annoyed if it is interrupted, nor do
they neglect their duties for its sake. The young are pleased
with praise from the old, and the old are delighted with respect
from the young. they remember their former acts with pleasure,
and are happy to perform their present jobs with success.
Through my influence, they are dear to the gods, beloved by
their friends, and honoured by their city and country. And when
the destined end of life arrives, they do not lie in despair and
oblivion, but, celebrated with words of praise, they flourish
forever in the hearts of mankind.*

*'By living in this way, young Hercules, you may secure the
most exalted happiness.'*

Socrates said, 'Anyway, that's how Prodicus told the story,
embellishing it with far more magnificent language than I can
give. You would be wise, Aristippus, to reflect on these
thoughts, and to pay more attention to the concerns of the
future period of your life.'

5

THE PROSTITUTE'S HELPER

A beautiful woman named Theodata had come to live in the city. All of the wealthy men, young and old, pursued her, and sculptors and painters vied to capture her striking looks.

One day, Cebes, one of Socrates' associates, came running up to him, exclaiming that he had just seen Theodata in the street and that her beauty was beyond description. Socrates, a lover of beauty, was intrigued.

'We should go and see her,' he said, 'because it's impossible to conceive just by hearing what a beauty that is beyond description can be like.'

He turned to me.

'What do you think, General? Should we organise a scouting party?'

I said I would be delighted to go, but didn't know where the lady lived. But Cebes was quickly on top of that, saying, 'You can't be too swift in following me,' and he scampered off with a laugh.

The five of us trotted after him and arrived at Theodata's house, where Socrates' name gained us admittance. When we entered Simmias held back and blushed, and remembering Aristippus' remark, I said to him, 'Don't worry, Aristippus says it's not the going in that's dangerous, but being unable to come out again.'

Socrates took his arm and we all trooped in. The house was richly furnished, and we were offered wine and fruit by

Theodata's servants, who were all young and attractive women.

When we were finally led into Theodata's room we all stopped and stared; Socrates' popped-out eyes were extended even more than usual. She was posing for a painter, and we were all drawn to her exposed figure, which, like her face, was indeed extremely beautiful. While the painter finished his work, Socrates said to us:

'My friends, should we feel obliged to Theodata for having shown us her beauty, or should she feel obliged to us for having viewed it with such admiration?

'If the exhibition of her body is of advantage to her, shouldn't she feel grateful to us, or if the sight has given us more pleasure, should we feel grateful to her?

'We are now praising Theodata, and when we speak of her beauty to others, she will gain profit as well. But for us, we now desire to embrace what we are seeing, and we shall go away in a state of excitement, and yearn for her when we are away. The natural consequence of this is that we shall be her adorers, and she will be worshipped as our mistress.'

Theodata, overhearing this, spoke up.

'If what you say, Socrates, is correct, I must be grateful for your coming up to see me. And now, if you'll excuse me, I need to change into something less comfortable. Do wait and make yourself at home.'

Later she returned, very expensively attired, accompanied by her mother in a richly ornamented dress, and several lovely female attendants.

Seeing that her house was so richly furnished, and she had such beautiful clothes and jewels, Socrates said to her, 'Tell me, Theodata, do you own an estate?'

'Unfortunately, no,' she said.

'Then perhaps you own a house that brings you income?'

'Not a house, either.'

'Do you own any slaves that make handicrafts?'

'No, I have no slaves.'

'Then how do you live?'

'If someone becomes my friend, and is willing to help me, he is my means of subsistence.'

'By Zeus, Theodata, then he is an excellent acquisition to you. It is much better to have a flock of friends than one of sheep or goats. But do you leave it to chance whether a friend, like a fly, will wing his way to you, or do you use any contrivance to attract them?'

'And how can I find a contrivance for such a purpose?'

'Much more readily, I would have thought, than spiders can. You know how spiders survive: they weave fine nets, and feed on whatever falls into them.'

'Do you think I should weave a net?'

'Yes I do, for you shouldn't expect that you will catch friends, the most valuable prey that can be taken, without some skill. Don't you know how much skill hunters use to catch hares, an animal that is worth much less than your friends.'

'Do tell, it sounds fascinating.'

'Because hares eat at night, the hunters bring night-hunting dogs to chase them. Since the hares hide during the day, the hunters bring on other dogs, which smell the route the hares have taken from feeding places to their burrows, and trace them out. As the hares are very swift, they have yet other dogs, also of great speed, that can catch them. And because some of the hares escape even from these dogs, they stretch nets across the paths through which they flee, to entangle them.'

'Then how should I use such skills to catch my friends?'

'If, instead of a dog, you could find someone who would track and discover the wealthy lovers of beauty, and, when he has found them, to contrive to drive them into your waiting nets.'

'And just exactly what nets do I have?'

'You have at least one, the one with which you closely

embrace your prey, and that is your body. In that body you have a mind by which you understand how you can gratify a man by merely gazing at him, and what you can whisper in his ear to cheer him up, and to learn that you should happily welcome the man who shows concern for you, and to shut out the ones who are insolent. You must attend carefully on a friend who is ill, to rejoice greatly with one who has succeeded in anything honourable, and to cherish affection in your whole soul to the one who sincerely cares for you. To love, I am sure you know, not only tenderly, but with true kindness of heart. Your friends try to please you, I know, because you try to bond with them, not with words only, but by your behaviour towards them.'

'I'm afraid, Socrates, that I use none of these schemes.'

'But Theodata, it's of the greatest importance to deal with a man according to his disposition, and with careful judgement. By serving and pleasing him the animal is easily taken and becomes completely attached to you.'

Theodata considered this and nodded, 'I admit that what you say is true.'

Socrates carried on, 'It makes sense, therefore, to request of your lovers only such favours as they will perform with the least cost to themselves. You must then make a return by obliging them as freely as they oblige you. Thus they will become most sincerely attached to you, and will love you longest and benefit you the most.

'But you will please them the most if you offer them your favours only when they ask for them. You see, even the most delicious meat, if a person offers it to someone before they have acquired an appetite for it, appears distasteful. In someone who is satisfied it can even excite loathing. But if one offers food to someone after having raised their appetite, it seems, even if it is very ordinary, extremely delectable.'

'Socrates, since you seem to be so knowledgeable about this, why don't you become my helper in securing friends? You would be extremely well rewarded.'

'I would be very happy to take on the job, if you can only persuade me.'

'And how can I persuade you?'

'I am sure that you can seek and find the means to do so, if you feel you need me.'

'Then I insist that you must come up often to visit me.'

'Unfortunately, Theodata, it's not easy for me to find leisure time. My own numerous occupations, both private and public, allow me no rest. I too have many friends, who do not allow me to leave them either during the day or night, learning from me many love charms and incantations.'

'Do you have knowledge of those arts, Socrates?'

'By what other influence do you think that Apollodorus here, and Xenophon, never leave my side? And through what other influence do you suppose that Cebes and Simmias have come to me from far away Thebes? I assure you, such effects were not produced without many love charms, incantations and magic birds.'

'I would be thrilled if you would show me your magic bird, Socrates, so that I can put it into action, and I will direct it first against you!'

'The problem, Theodata, is that I don't want to be drawn to you, so much as that you should be drawn to me.'

'Well, then, I will come to you, Socrates, but only if you take care to let me in.'

'I will let you in, Theodata, so long as there is not another more acceptable than you already inside.'

'You mean, I have a rival?'

'There is already someone deep inside me who has a prior claim, Theodata. And this is someone who guards my every thought, and directs my every action, so that I am reluctant to displace him.'

'A pity,' she said. 'We could have made an interesting team.'

6

MY FIRST BREAK

*In Which Xenephon Becomes
A Cavalry Commander*

I met up with Socrates in the marketplace. As usual, he was surrounded by a small group of associates, and I had to wait all afternoon for him to be by himself. I asked him if we could talk, and he suggested I accompany him home.

Once I told him the news that I had been selected as a cavalry commander, he was delighted for me, but wanted to know why I particularly wanted to be a commander?

'It can't be for the sake of riding at the head of the cavalry, since the horse-archers are given that role and they ride in front of the commander.'

'That's right,' I said.

'And I'm sure it isn't merely for the sake of being noticed, for a common madman is noticed by everyone.'

'You're correct.'

'Is it, General, that you hope to improve the cavalry and if the need for the services of the cavalry arises, you hope, as their leader, to provide some benefit to the state?'

'That's what I hope, certainly.'

'And it will be an achievement for you, if you are able to do that. But is it your job to look after both horses and their riders?'

'That's right.'

'Then, General, tell me first how it is you intend to improve the horses?'

'Well, I don't think that is my business. I think that each man must take care of his own horse.'

'But what if some of the men bring their horses to you so diseased in the hooves, or weak in the legs, or so undernourished that they are not able to follow your lead? And what if others have horses so unmanageable that they are not able to maintain the position you give them? And if others have steeds so vicious that you cannot position them at all? What would be the use to you of such a cavalry? And how would you be able, as their commander, to be of any service to your country?'

'This is good advice, Socrates, so I will try to look after the horses as far as I am able.'

'Will you also try to make the riders better?'

'Of course.'

'Will you first of all make them more expert in mounting their horses?'

'I ought to, since if any of them fall off, they would be better prepared to remount.'

'And if you have to fight a battle, will you try to entice your enemy to a nice smooth, level, sand-strewn spot, like your training ground, or will you force your men to practise on any kind of ground, on which the enemy may appear?'

'The latter would be better.'

'Will you also take care that the greatest possible number of your men will be able to hurl the javelin while on horseback?'

'That would be a good idea.'

'And have you considered how to increase the courage of your cavalry, since you will want to make them more courageous and incite them against the enemy?'

'I have not yet considered it, but I will now try to do so.'

'And have you thought about how you will get your cavalry to obey you, General? For without obedience you will have no profit either from horse or rider, no matter how spirited and valiant they may be.'

'You're right, Socrates, but what means can a commander use to most effectively get them to obey?'

'No doubt you're aware that in all circumstances people most willingly obey those whom they consider most able to direct them. In sickness patients obey the one who they think is the best doctor. On board ship, they obey the person they consider to be the best pilot, and in agriculture people follow the one they consider the best cultivator.'

'Unquestionably,' I said.

'Isn't it likely, then, that in horsemanship also, others will be most willing to obey the one who appears to know best what should be done?'

'So if, Socrates, I were to appear as the best rider of them all, will that circumstance be sufficient to induce them to obey me?'

'If you can also convince them, General, that it is best and safest for them to obey you.'

'And how do I do that?'

'This is an easier thing to do than if you had, like a Sophist, to convince them that bad things are better and more profitable than good ones.'

'Do you mean,' I said, 'that a commander of cavalry, in addition to his other qualifications, needs to acquire some ability in speech?'

'General, do you think you can command your cavalry by silence? Haven't you realised, that whatever excellent principles we have learned by our civilisation, principles by which we know how to live, we learned only through the medium of speech. Whatever valuable instruction any person acquires, he also acquires them by means of speech.

'Don't those who teach best use speech the most? And those who know the most important truths are able to discuss them with the greatest eloquence?

'Why else do I sit here in the marketplace every day talking to people like you and Plato and Simmias? Isn't it through speech that I try to communicate some knowledge and wisdom to you? And when you understand what I say to you, and act according to the knowledge that you have acquired, don't I praise you, General, for your good sense?'

'You do,' I said.

'And don't you feel good when I praise you for having learned something?'

'I do.'

'And don't you then want to learn some more? There is nothing an Athenian likes more than to be praised. We are an ambitious nation, and ambition is the greatest incitement to excellence and honour. An Athenian will always want to be honoured and noticed for doing something well.

'So if you want to improve the Athenian cavalry, and to make them excel in every way, you must praise them when they do well. In this way you can excite your men to their best efforts both to benefit them, yourself and your countrymen.'

This is why Socrates never wrote a book, or even left behind one written word. He taught us in two ways, of which the first, as he said, was through speech. The second was through his actions, his way of living and being. He was a philosopher because of his very existence, and in both speech and action he had only the desire to communicate the truths that he could help us discover. And these truths he gave freely to us, only wishing that we would put into effect the good teaching that he gave us.

7

CRITO'S PROTECTOR

*In Which Socrates Solves
A Problem for Crito*

Crito was Socrates' oldest friend, and they grew up together in the same neighbourhood. Crito was a successful farmer and he once mentioned to Socrates how difficult it was for a man to live in Athens and mind his own business, because of the many sycophants and informers who harassed the rich, in the belief that such activities helped to support the democracy.

While having Socrates to dinner at his house, he told him, 'At this very moment, there are people bringing actions against me in court, not because they have suffered any wrong from me, but because they think that I would rather pay them off than have the trouble of fighting them in court.'

Socrates considered the problem and said to him, 'Tell me, Crito, don't you have dogs to drive wolves away from your sheep?'

'I do, because it is more profitable to keep them than not to.'

'Wouldn't you then be inclined to keep a man also, who would be willing and able to drive away from you these informers that are molesting you?'

'I would with pleasure, if I were not afraid that he would also turn against me.'

'But don't you see,' said Socrates, 'that it would be much more pleasant for him to help himself by assisting such a man as you, than by incurring your enmity. And be assured that there are such people here in Athens, who would be extremely ambitious to have you as a friend.'

Following this discussion, Socrates pointed Crito in the direction of Archedemus, a man of great ability both in speaking and acting, but who was poor; for he was not the kind of person who was willing to make money from any means going, but was a lover of honesty, and a man of superior mind.

Archedemus quickly discovered that Crito's current tormentor had often abused the law and made many enemies, so he sought out some of the people who had suffered at his hands. With them he brought the informer to a public trial, at which it would be settled what punishment he should suffer or what fine to pay. The sycophant, conscious of his guilt, tried every means to get out of the hands of Archedemus; but Archedemus was like a leech and would not let go until the informer agreed to stop bothering Crito, and paid him some money as well.

In this way Archedemus was able to get the better of the sycophants and extract money from them, rather than allow them to exploit Crito. In return, whenever Crito gathered in his corn, or oil, wine or wool, he used to take a portion of it and give it to Archedemus; and he used to invite him to his sacrifices and feasts, and paid him respect in many other ways.

Once Archedemus had succeeded in this task, and some other jobs as well, then, as when any shepherd has a good dog, other shepherds would like to place their own flocks near him, in order to have the benefit of this dog, so likewise many of the rich friends of Crito begged him to lend them the services of Archedemus as a protector.

Archedemus willingly acceded to Crito in this respect, and thus not only Crito himself, but his friends as well, were left in peace. And if any of those with whom he had a problem taunted Archedemus with receiving favours from Crito, and paying court to him, Archedemus would ask, 'Is it disgraceful to be benefited by honest men, and to make them your friends by serving them in return, and being in opposition to the unprincipled. Or is it better to make the honourable and good your enemies by trying to wrong them, and to make the bad your friends by co-operating with them, and associate with criminals instead of the virtuous?'

From this time on, Archedemus became one of Crito's friends, and was honoured by the other friends of Crito, and all because of the practical wisdom of Socrates.

THE ART OF
GOVERNING

8

Socrates did not get involved in politics if he could avoid it, but he thought it was his duty to help young men who were interested in careers in government to discover how they must act to achieve any measure of success.

When Plato's brother Glaucon was still a teenager, he began to harangue the people because of his desire to have a share in the government. Because he was so young, he was constantly being dragged down from the Tribunal, and none of his friends or relatives could prevent him from making himself look ridiculous. Plato's family asked Socrates to try to dissuade Glaucon from trying again, and he did it in this way.

Early one spring morning I saw Socrates making his way at a fast pace up to the Assembly, and since this was not one of his usual haunts I was curious as to why he was going there. Catching up with him I asked if something was the matter. Continuing to walk quickly he turned back to see who had greeted him.

'General, it's good to see you. Come with me, there's no problem, but perhaps you might learn something.'

So I caught up with him as he wandered around the Assembly entrance, clearly looking for someone. At last he came in sight of his prey, and, slowing his walk to a more leisurely amble, he greeted Glaucon as if their meeting was a total accident.

After greeting each other, Socrates said to him, 'Glaucon,

I understand you've decided to govern the state for us.'

'I have, Socrates,' he said.

'That is a substantial position for one so young, but it's certain that if you achieve your ambition, you will be able to secure for yourself whatever you desire, and will be able to benefit your friends. You can build up your father's house, and increase the power of your country. You will become celebrated, first of all in your own city, and afterwards throughout Greece, and perhaps even among the barbarians. Wherever you go, you will be an object of general admiration.'

On hearing this, Glaucon looked extremely satisfied with himself and was happy to stay and listen.

Socrates went on to say, 'But it's plain, Glaucon, that if you wish to be lauded like this, you must benefit the state.'

'Certainly,' Glaucon answered.

'Then please, in the name of the gods, don't hide from us how you intend to act, but inform us what actions you will take to benefit us?'

At this Glaucon blinked several times and was strangely silent, as if considering what he should say. So Socrates broke the silence, 'For example, just as if you wished to help the family of a friend, by making them richer, tell me whether you will in the same way also endeavour to make the state richer?'

'Of course,' he said confidently.

'Would it be richer if its revenues were increased?'

'Very likely.'

'Then tell me from what activities the revenues of the state arise, and how much they total. No doubt you've already considered this in case any revenues fall short, and how you would be able to make up the deficiency.'

'These matters I have not yet considered,' said Glaucon rather quietly.

'Well,' said Socrates, 'if you have not had time to consider this point, tell me at least the annual expenditure of the state.

Undoubtedly you intend to save whatever is superfluous in it.'

'Indeed, I have been too busy to turn my attention to that subject either.'

'Alright, we'll put off making the state richer for the moment. But Glaucon, I don't see how it is possible for someone who is ignorant of its expenditure and income to manage these matters?'

'But Socrates,' countered Glaucon, 'it's possible to enrich the state at the expense of our enemies, by taking their money.'

'Extremely possible, indeed, if we are stronger than they. But if we are weaker, we may lose everything that we have.'

'What you say is true,' said Glaucon dejectedly.

'Accordingly, the ruler who deliberates about going to war ought to know the force both of his own country and of the enemy, so that, if his own country is superior to that of the enemy, he may advise it to enter the war, but, if inferior, he may persuade it to be cautious of doing so.'

'Absolutely,' said Glaucon energetically. He was perking up.

'So then, Glaucon, tell us the strength of the country by land and sea, and also that of the enemy.'

'I can't just tell you that off the top of my head, Socrates.'

'I see. Well, if you have it written down, bring it, for I would be extremely glad to hear what it is.'

'To tell the truth, I have not yet written it down.'

'Then let's put off considerations of war for the time being. It's very likely that, on account of the magnitude of these subjects, and as you are just commencing your administration, you have not yet looked into them. But to the defence of the country, I am quite sure you have directed your attention, and you know how many garrisons are in an advantageous position, and how many men would be sufficient to maintain them, and that you will advise your countrymen to make the garrisons in advantageous positions stronger and to remove the useless ones.'

'By Zeus, I will recommend that we remove them all, since they keep such negligent guard that property is secretly carried off out of the country.'

'But Glaucon, if we remove the garrisons, don't you think that license will be given to anyone that wants to pillage? Have you actually gone yourself and examined into this fact, or how is it you know that the garrisons conduct themselves with such negligence?'

'I form my own opinions.'

'Perhaps we should also settle these matters when we no longer count on opinion, but on certain knowledge?'

'Perhaps that is the better course.'

'To the silver mines, however, I know that you have not gone, so as to tell us why a smaller revenue is coming from that source now than came a few years ago.'

'I have not gone there yet.'

'Indeed, I understand that the place is so unhealthy that, when it is necessary to bring it under consideration, this can be a sufficient excuse for you.'

'Now you're joking with me, Socrates.'

'I am, Glaucon, you're right. But seriously, I am sure you have not neglected to consider, but have calculated, how long the grain, which is produced in the country, will suffice to maintain the city and how much it requires for the year, in order that the city may not suffer from scarcity. From your own knowledge you will be able, by giving advice concerning the necessaries of life, to support and preserve the city.'

'Socrates, you propose a vast field for me, if it will be necessary for me to attend to so many subjects.'

'Nevertheless, Glaucon, a person cannot run a household properly, unless he or she knows everything that it requires, and takes care to supply it with everything necessary. Our city consists of more than ten thousand houses, and since it is difficult to provide for so many at once, how is it that you have not even tried to aid one first of all, for example that of your uncle, Charmides, which stands in need of some help?

If you are able to help that one, you may proceed to help more. But if you are unable to benefit even one, how will it be possible for you to benefit many?'

'Socrates, I would improve my uncle's house, if I could only persuade him to let me.'

'So, if you can't persuade your uncle, do you expect to make all the Athenians, together with your uncle, accept your arguments? Take care, Glaucon, that in your search to acquire glory, you don't meet the reverse of it. Don't you see how dangerous it is for a person to speak of, or undertake, something which he does not understand? Contemplate, among other people, those who plainly talk of, and attempt to do, what they do not know, and consider whether they appear to you, by such conduct, to obtain more applause or censure, whether they seem to be more admired or despised?

'Contemplate, also, those who have some understanding of what they say and do, and you will find, I think, in all transactions, those who are praised and admired are those who have the most knowledge, and those who incur censure and neglect are those that have least.

'If, therefore, you desire to gain esteem and reputation in your country, endeavour to succeed in gaining knowledge of what you wish to do. For if, when you excel others in this qualification, you proceed to manage the affairs of the state, I shall not be surprised if you very easily obtain what you desire.'

Glaucon took this advice to heart, and started to gain more information and knowledge about the affairs of the state. He stopped insisting that he be given some power and instead asked more questions about revenues, defence and supplies and listened carefully to the answers.

9

A LESSON IN WISDOM

*In Which Xenephon Learns
About Happiness*

Socrates asked me, 'Do you want to do well, General? And by do well, I mean, be successful and find happiness?'

'I think everyone wants to be successful and find happiness, Socrates.'

'Good. So, given that everyone wants to do well, be successful and find happiness, the obvious question is, "How can we get it?" Is it by having plenty of good things?'

'Yes.'

'OK. So what kinds of things are good things? It doesn't take a genius to work that out, does it? I mean, everyone would say that it's good to be rich, right?'

'Right.'

'And the same to be healthy, beautiful, and have a fit body?'

'Sure.'

'And we shouldn't forget a good parentage, power and status in one's country, which are also obviously good.'

'I agree.'

'Have we missed anything? What about self-control, integrity and courage? Can we class these as good? Not everyone would. What would you say, General?'

'I would say they are good.'

'Fine. And how about wisdom?'

'Also good.'

'Excellent. Now, let's be sure that we haven't forgotten anything that's good?'

'I think that's it, Socrates.'

Then Socrates looked up, shook his head, and said, 'I'm sorry, General, but I think we've forgotten the most important good of all.'

'Which one?'

'Good luck, which everyone – even the most uneducated – thinks is the greatest good of all. On the other hand, maybe good luck is redundant.'

'Why is that?'

'Because if we add good luck to the list we are really adding something which has already been included, and so we'd be covering the same point twice.'

'What do you mean?'

'Well, I believe that wisdom is good luck, so to me it's already been included.'

I was surprised at this, and couldn't quite follow the argument, so Socrates jumped in to help me,

'Don't you think that flute-players have the best luck with success at flute-playing?'

'I do.'

'And the same goes for scribes as regards reading and writing?'

'Yes.'

'And surely you wouldn't expect anyone to have better luck, when facing danger at sea, than an expert pilot, generally speaking?'

'No.'

'And would you prefer to face military risks and hazards under a clever or an ignorant commander?'

'You know my answer to that one.'

'And would you rather take your chances with a wise or ignorant doctor when you are ill?'

'Wise.'

'So, do you think that you would have better luck if your affairs were handled by an expert rather than an ignoramus?'

'An expert, obviously.'

'Therefore, in all areas of life, wisdom causes people to enjoy good fortune. Wisdom can never fail, but must be successful and attain its goal, otherwise it would no longer be wisdom. So, I think that if we include wisdom as a good, then there is no need to also include good luck.'

'I'll accept that.'

'Good. So now, where were we? We had agreed that if we had many good things, then we would be happy and successful?'

'That's it.'

'Now, would we happy if we had no benefit from possessing all these good things? Or do they have to benefit us?'

'I'd say they have to benefit us, otherwise they are not good.'

'So, does just having something without using it benefit us? For example, if we had lots of food and drink, but didn't actually eat or drink it, would we benefit from it?'

'Of course not.'

'Now, let's take a craftsman who has all the tools for his job, but doesn't use them. Is he going to be successful, just because he has in his possession everything he needs? For example, a carpenter who has wood and tools, but doesn't actually do any carpentry, is he going to benefit from having them?'

'Not really.'

'And how about if someone has acquired wealth and all the other good things on our list, but doesn't use them. Would just possessing all these things provide happiness?'

'Of course not.'

'So it follows that to be happy one has to not only have possession of these things, but to use them. No benefit is gained by possession alone.'

'That sounds right.'

'So if we have possession of good things and use them, does this constitute a sufficient condition of happiness?'

'I would say so.'

'But for this to be the case, do they need to be used correctly, or not?'

'Correctly, I would say.'

'I agree with that. I would say that it's better for something to be left alone rather than used incorrectly, since the one is neutral, while the other is positively bad. Isn't this our position?'

'It is.'

'Now, when we work with and use wood, it is knowledge of carpentry that produces correct use, isn't it?'

'Of course.'

'And if we work with tools and equipment, is it knowledge again that produces correct use?'

'Yes.'

'Now, when we use the good things that we talked about – wealth, beauty, health – is it knowledge which governs our actions and makes them correct, or is it something else?'

'It's knowledge.'

'Then, can we say that it's knowledge that gives people success and happiness, as well as giving them good luck, in whatever they possess or do?'

'We can.'

'So can we honestly say that if a person lacks wisdom and intelligence, that person will still benefit from their other possessions? Which is better: to be rich in possessions and full of activities, but without much intelligence, or to have fewer possessions and do less with more sense? We can look at it this way: the less a person does, the fewer mistakes to be made. The fewer mistakes, the less unsuccessful that person will be. And the less unsuccessful, the less miserable. Do you think this is so?'

'I do.'

'Who would be more likely to do less – a rich person or a poor one?'

'A poor one.'

'A weak person or a strong one?'

'A weak one.'

'A somebody or a nobody.'

'A nobody.'

'And do courage and self-reliance produce less activity, or does cowardice?'

'Cowardice.'

'So laziness rather than energy?'

'Agreed.'

'And walking rather than running? Dull senses rather than sharp ones?'

'Yes to all.'

'Summing up, General, it seems likely that our original list of all the things that we said were good was not concerned with the *sense* in which they are naturally good in themselves. No, the facts seem to be like this: if ignorance rules them, they are greater evils than their opposites, to the extent that they put more power in the hands of their evil leader. But if they are directed by wisdom and intelligence, they become greater goods – but in themselves, what we call "good" and "bad" things have no inherent value.'

'I think you must be right, Socrates.'

'So what have we learned from all this? Is it that of the things we have been discussing, only wisdom is good and only ignorance is bad, and nothing else is either good or bad, but is neutral?'

'I think so.'

'Unfortunately, General, our investigation is not quite at an end. We said that the desire for happiness is universal and we discovered that happiness depends on use – correct use – of things, and that correctness and good luck, are themselves the products of knowledge. Now if this is so, it follows that

everyone should be putting all their efforts into making themselves as wise as possible, doesn't it?'

'Yes.'

'Now, take someone who thinks that wisdom is a far more
valuable gift to receive than money – especially from their
parents, but also from anyone they like or admire, and from
strangers and neighbours – and that person begs and pleads
with them to share their wisdom. For someone like that,
General, with their mind set on a goal of wisdom, is it
demeaning or a source of blame to be dominated by, and
enslaved to, a lover or anyone else, and, in order to become
wise, to be willing to perform any worthwhile act of service?
Do you think this is so?'

'I think it's right.'

'I am right if wisdom is something that can be taught,
General, and not something that people get by chance. But
that's another problem that you and I have not yet gotten to
grips with, and reached a verdict on.'

'Well, *I* think wisdom can be taught, Socrates.'

Socrates smiled.

'I'm glad to hear it, General. Thanks for letting me off
from a very long inquiry into precisely that question, whether
or not wisdom can be taught. So, if you think it can be taught,
and it's the sole source of happiness and good luck, then
wouldn't you say that philosophy is essential, since philosophy is the love of wisdom?'

'I do think it is the most essential thing, Socrates.'

Socrates asked me if I knew why wisdom was of supreme
importance to him and to all Athenians. When I could give
no satisfactory answer, he told me the story of Athena:

*Athena was the goddess of wisdom and she became the
favourite child of Zeus.*

*Her mother was Metis, the goddess of prudence, who was
Zeus's first wife. He depended on her because he needed her
wise counsel, but Mother Earth warned him that Metis was*

pregnant and if she were to have a son by him, this son would dethrone him. Zeus didn't want to lose his power, but he also could not do without Metis' sage advice.

He thought of a cunning plan, and asked her to play a game of changing shapes with him. She forgot her prudence and started to change herself into various animals and other creatures. Just as she exuberantly changed from an elephant to a fly, Zeus opened his mouth and swallowed her! Ever since that time, Metis has sat in Zeus's head and guided him with good advice from that place.

Now it turned out that Metis was in fact expecting a daughter, and so the expectant mother started to hammer out a helmet and to make a beautiful gown for her new child. Soon Zeus began to complain of pounding headaches and he finally cried out in agony. The other gods came to help him, and the skilled Hephaestus took his tools and split open his father's skull to relieve his pain. Out sprang Zeus's daughter Athena, fully grown, her grey eyes flashing, wearing the helmet and gown her mother had made for her. Thunder roared and the gods stood in awe.

Athena's constant companion was Nike, the spirit of victory. With Nike at her side, Athena led armies, but only those that fought for justice. In times of peace she stood beside the artists of Greece and taught them the fine and useful arts.

After some time there arose a settlement in Greece that soon grew into a city. Athena and her uncle Poseidon were both fond of this place, and after a long quarrel, they decided that the one who gave it the finest gift would have it for their own.

Leading a procession of citizens, the two gods mounted the Acropolis, the flat-topped rock that crowned the city. Poseidon struck the cliff with his trident, and a spring welled up. The people were amazed and grateful, but when they tasted the water their wonder turned to disappointment because it was salty. Since Poseidon was the god of the sea, his springs would always be salty and of little use.

Then Athena stepped forward and gave the city her gift. She planted an olive tree on the rock, the first one they had ever seen. The people said that Athena's tree was the best gift, since it gave them food, oil and wood. And so the city was hers. They built her a beautiful temple on top of the Acropolis so that she could watch over her new city, which was called Athens in her honour. Accompanied by the wise owl, her bird, which stood on her shoulder, she inspired and led the city to fame for its arts and crafts.

'And so, General, wisdom leads our city and must forever be its guardian. That is why we need to constantly consider it, discuss it, understand it and live by it. Do you understand, General?'

'I do,' I said.

'Good, and will you be taking it up?'

'To the best of my ability.'

'I couldn't ask for anything more, General.'

10

ARISTODEMUS AND
THE GODS

*S*ocrates heard that little Aristodemus did not sacrifice to the gods, or pray to them, or use divination, but instead ridiculed those who did. This offended Socrates, who was truly pious and believed in the existence of gods. I was with Socrates one day when he came across Aristodemus.

Socrates greeted him, 'Tell me, Aristodemus, do you admire anyone for their genius?'

'I do,' he replied.

'Can you tell us who they are?'

'In epic poetry I admire Homer, in tragedy, Sophocles, in sculpture, Polycletus, and in painting, Zeuxis.'

'And who would you say is more worthy of admiration, an artist who creates stiff and motionless images, or one who forms figures endowed with sense and life?'

'I would say those who create living images, since they produce them not by chance, but by intelligence.'

'There are some things whose purpose is uncertain, while others evidently exist for some useful purpose. Which of the two would you say were made by chance, and which by intelligence?'

'Obviously those which exist for some useful purpose must be the results of intelligence.'

'Then, doesn't also the power that first made people appear to have given them, for some useful purpose, those parts by which they perceive different objects – the eyes to see, the ears to hear? What would be the use of smells if we were not given any nostrils? What perception would there have been of sweet and sour, and of every pleasing taste, if a tongue had not been formed?

'In addition to these, doesn't it seem to you like the work of forethought, to guard the eyes, since they are so delicate, with eyelids like doors, which when it's necessary to see are opened, but which can close for sleep? To make eyelashes grow like a screen to protect against winds? To provide eyebrows above the eyes so that sweat pouring down the forehead may not annoy them?

'To ensure that the ears can receive all kinds of sounds, yet are never blocked? And that the front teeth of all animals are adapted to cut, and the back teeth to receive food from them and to grind it? To place the mouth, through which animals take in what they desire, near the eyes and nose? And since what passes out of the stomach is offensive, to turn this away, and remove it as far as possible from the senses? Can you doubt whether such an arrangement of things, made so apparently with attention, can be the result of chance or of intelligence?'

'Looked at in this light, Socrates, they do appear like the work of some maker who studied the welfare of animals.'

'And to have engendered in them a love of having offspring, and in mothers a desire to rear their young, and to have implanted in the young a desire for life, and the greatest fear of death?'

'I must admit these do appear to be the contrivances of someone who designed that animals should continue to exist.'

'Do you also think that you have some portion of intelligence?'

'Question me, and you will find the answer.'

'Do you suppose that nothing intelligent exists anywhere else? When you know that you have in your body only a small portion of the Earth, which is vast, and a small portion of water, which is also vast, and that your body is made so that you receive only a tiny portion of other things which are also vast, do you think that you have obtained for yourself, by some extraordinary good fortune, the only intelligence that exists, and that this collection of vast bodies, earthly and celestial, countless in numbers, is maintained in order by something devoid of reason?'

'I can hardly suppose that there exists a ruling intelligence among this collection of bodies, since I cannot see the directors, as I see the agents of things that are done here on Earth.'

'Nor do you see your own soul, which is the director of your body; so that, by similar reasoning, you may say that you yourself do nothing with understanding or intelligence, but everything by chance.'

'Socrates,' replied Aristodemus, 'don't misunderstand me. I do not despise the gods, but I consider them as too exalted to need my attention.'

'But,' said Socrates, 'the more exalted they are, when they stoop to attend to you, the more ought you to honour them.'

'I assure you,' replied Aristodemus, 'that if I believed the gods took any thought for people, I would not neglect them.'

'Don't you believe the gods take thought for people? The gods have made man alone, of all animals, erect (which erect posture enabled us to look ahead to a greater distance, and to contemplate better what is above, and makes those parts less liable to injury in which the gods have placed the eyes, and ears, and mouth). And they have given the other animals only feet, which merely enables them to walk and run, while to us they have added hands, which execute most of the things through which we are better off than they.

'And though all animals have tongues, the gods have made that of man alone of such a nature, as by touching sometimes one part of the mouth, and sometimes another, to express articulate sounds, and to signify everything that we wish to communicate to others. Do you not see, too, that to other animals they limited the pleasures of sexual congress to a certain season of the year, but they allow this to us uninterruptedly into old age?

'Nor did it satisfy the gods to take care of only the body, but what is most important of all, they implanted in us the soul, our most excellent part. For what other animal has a soul which understands, first of all, that the gods, who have arranged such a vast and noble order of things, exist? What other species of animal, besides man, offers worship to the gods? What other animal has a mind better equipped to guard against hunger or thirst, or cold or heat, or to relieve disease, or to acquire strength through exercise, and to study to obtain knowledge; or is more capable of remembering whatever it has heard or seen or learned?

'Isn't it clearly evident to you, that, in comparison to all other animals, people live like gods, excelling them by nature, both in body and mind? For if an animal like an ox had the intelligence of a person, it would be unable to carry out the things it could conceive; and animals which have hands, but are unable to reason, have no advantage over others; and do you, who share both these excellent endowments, think that the gods have taken no thought for you? What do they have to do, before you will think that they have given you some thought?'

'I will think so,' observed Aristodemus, 'when they send me, as you tell us they send you, a guide to show me what I ought and ought not to do.'

'But when the gods send messages to the Athenians by means of divination, do you not believe that the message is for you also? Or when they give warnings to the Greeks by sending portents, do they except you alone from the human race, and utterly neglect you?

'Do you suppose that the gods would have engendered a belief in people that they are able to benefit or injure them, unless they were really able to do so, and that people, if they had been thus so perpetually deluded, would not have become sensible of this delusion? Don't you see that the oldest and wisest human communities, the oldest and wisest cities and nations, are the most respectful of the gods, and that the wisest age of man is the most observant of their worship?

'Consider also,' continued Socrates, 'that your mind, existing with your body, directs your body as it pleases; and it is fitting therefore to believe that the intelligence pervading all things directs all things as may be agreeable to it, and not to think that while your eyes can extend its sight over many miles, that of the divine power is unable to see all things at once, or that while your mind can think of things here, as well as in Sicily or Egypt, that the mind of the deity is incapable of regarding everything in existence at the same time.

'If you discover, by giving attention to people, those who are willing to be attentive to you in return, and, by doing favours for people, those who are willing to return your favours, and just as, by asking people for advice, you discover who is wise, you should, in the same way, make a trial or test of the gods by offering worship to them, and see if they will in turn offer you advice concerning things hidden from other people. You will then discover that the divinity is of such a power and of such a nature, as to see and hear all things at once, to be present everywhere, and to have a care and thought for all things at the same time.'

By delivering such thoughts, Socrates seems to me to have led his associates to refrain from what was impious, unjust or dishonourable, not merely when they were in other people's presence, but even when they were utterly alone, since they would then conceive that nothing they did would escape the knowledge of the gods.

11

GOOD ADVICE

*In Which Socrates and Xenophon
Help a Friend in Trouble*

I grew up during the twenty-eight-year war between Sparta and Athens, which ended in a disastrous defeat for my country. The victorious Spartans took control of Athens and appointed a government of thirty oligarchs. This small cabal soon made themselves notorious for the vicious, lawless and arbitrary violence they perpetrated on their enemies, and they became known as the Thirty Tyrants.

The Tyrants allowed three thousand of their friends to live in Athens, but everyone else had to leave. Many of us fled to the port of Piraeus, five miles away, where the defenders of democracy eventually began a war against the supporters of the oligarchy.

During this period Socrates and I were both living in Piraeus, and late one afternoon I was going to his house to join him for dinner. On the way I noticed his friend Aristarchus wandering around, looking miserable and distracted. I wondered if he was ill, so when I got to the house I told Socrates what I thought.

Socrates was concerned, and asked me to take him to the place where I saw Aristarchus. After wandering around, and asking some people who knew him, we finally located him sitting at one of the harbours, looking dejectedly out at sea.

Socrates was the first to get to him, and he put his hand on his friend's shoulder,

'Aristarchus, you look terribly worried. What's wrong?'

He perked up on seeing us, 'Socrates! Xenophon! – so glad to see you!' But then his face fell again, as if his problems were too much to bear.

'I'm in terrible trouble. Ever since this damn war started my relatives have fled here, and my surviving sisters, nieces and cousins have taken up residence in my house! I now have living with me fourteen freeborn people, plus all their slaves.

'At the same time, I'm not getting any revenue from my lands, since the enemy has taken possession of them. I can't get any rent from my houses, since there are so few people living in Athens, and I can't sell any furniture, because there are no buyers.'

Socrates commiserated with him, 'This doesn't sound good, Aristarchus.'

Aristarchus agreed, 'The worst part is that I'm afraid my relatives will die, since I can't feed them all under these conditions.'

He looked completely lost, like a man who had nowhere to turn for help.

Socrates looked thoughtful. 'Surely there has to be a solution to your problem.' He looked around at the people on the harbour-side, noticed someone, and pointed him out to us.

'Look at Ceramon over there. He also supports a large number of people, but not only is he able to provide enough money for himself and them, but he makes so much as to be positively rich! And you're afraid that you will all die of hunger!'

'I'm sure Ceramon has many slaves working for him, while I have to support well-born people,' said Aristarchus.

'And which of the two do you consider to be better,' asked Socrates, 'the freeborn who are with you, or the slaves who are with him?'

Without hesitation, Aristarchus replied, 'I consider the free-born to be better.'

Socrates nodded in agreement. 'Then don't you think it's a disgrace that he should become rich through inferior people, and that you should have so many problems, even though you live with those who are better?'

'It's a disgrace,' agreed Aristarchus, 'but it's not surprising, because he supports craftsmen and workers, while I have mainly women of discernment and education.'

Socrates paused. 'I see.' Aristarchus and I both looked at him expectantly. I could feel some philosophy coming on. Finally, Socrates broke the silence. 'Aristarchus, would you say craftsmen are people who know how to make something useful?'

'Of course!' he said.

'And would you say barley meal was useful?'

'Very.'

'And bread?'

'Of course.'

'And coats and cloaks?'

'Extremely useful.'

'And would you say the women living with you know how to make any of these things?'

'All of them, I would think.'

'Surely you're aware that from the manufacture of just one of these items, barley meal, Nausicydes supports not only himself and his household, but also earns so much that he even lends the government money?'

'I am.'

'And aren't you also aware that Cyrebus, by making bread, maintains his entire household, and lives in luxury; that Demea supports himself by making cloaks, Menon by making woollen ones, and that most of the Megarians live by making mantles?'

'I know all this, Socrates,' said Aristarchus, 'but they do it by buying barbarian slaves and forcing them to work hard. I happen to be stuck with freeborn relatives.'

Aristarchus sighed, and I could see his whole body seem to deflate. If his problem couldn't be solved it seemed to me that he would become seriously ill, or even suicidal. I decided I had to say something positive and practical.

'Just because they're freeborn and your relatives, doesn't mean that they should do nothing but eat and sleep?'

Socrates picked up on this. 'Xenophon is right, Aristarchus. Let me ask you this. Among other free persons, do you think that those who live in idleness, like your relatives do, spend their time more pleasantly, and are happier, than those who practise the skills they know, and which are useful to support life?'

Aristarchus considered the question, and nodded, 'No, I think those who work are generally happier.'

Socrates also nodded. 'Then, is it your experience that idleness and carelessness are helpful to mankind, either for learning important things, or for remembering what they have learned, or for maintaining the health of their bodies, or for acquiring and preserving what is essential for the support of life, and that work and discipline are of no use at all?'

'No, that's certainly not my experience.'

Socrates continued, 'And the skills which you say they know, would you say they learned them as being useless to maintain life, and with the intention of never practising them? Or, on the contrary, with a view to apply themselves to them, and to reap some benefit from them?'

Aristarchus rubbed his mouth and said, 'I'm not sure.'

Socrates tried another approach. 'Well then, in which condition do you think people will have more self-control, living in idleness, or having some useful employment? In which condition will they be more honest, if they work, or if they sit around, wondering about how to procure their next meal?'

Aristarchus knew the answer to this one. 'I would say in working.'

'Good. Now, in the present circumstances, I imagine, you

probably don't feel very close to your relatives because you find them a burden?'

Aristarchus smiled ruefully, 'To say the least.'

'And they must sense that you are annoyed at having to look after them. From such feelings there is the danger that dislike may grow stronger and stronger, and that previous friendly feelings will diminish, leading to mutual hatred.'

Aristarchus agreed, 'I think that is a very likely outcome.'

Socrates now pressed his point home, 'However, if you arrange things so that they can work, it will be easy for you to regain your affection for them, when you see how useful they are to you, and they in turn will grow closer to you, when they feel that you are happy at having them near you.'

Aristarchus protested, 'But, Socrates, I don't know if they want to be employed?'

'Aristarchus, if you were going to ask them to do anything dishonourable, death would be preferable; but the skills they know are, it appears, those that are very fit and respectable for women; everyone does what they know best with the greatest ease and facility, and with the utmost credit and pleasure. My suggestion is that you recommend to them this line of conduct, which will benefit both you and them; and I think that they will cheerfully agree with your wishes.'

Aristarchus looked relieved, as if he could finally see a way out of his dilemma. You could see his mind starting to work again, 'Socrates, I think this might work. Before, I didn't want to borrow money because I had no idea how I could repay it. But now I think I could manage a loan, so that I can buy the necessary materials to start work.'

So Aristarchus borrowed some money and bought some tools, cloth and materials. His relatives worked hard – even while eating their meals – and his house was turned into a factory. His looks changed from gloomy to cheerful, and instead of regarding each other with hatred, his relatives loved

Aristarchus as their protector, and he loved them because they were so useful to him.

Once all this was done, Aristarchus came to see Socrates at home, to thank him, and to tell him with delight of the state of things in his house. He looked a different person, lighter and happier.

Socrates was pleased to hear the news. 'So everything is fine now, Aristarchus? No one is starving?'

'No, no, it's all worked out very well. Money is positively rolling in.' Here his broad smile faded a little, and he carried on, a little apologetically.

'However, there is just one small problem. My relatives are working very hard, really diligently; but now they've begun to complain that I'm the only person in the house who doesn't lift a finger. What should I do?'

Socrates turned to me, and raised his eyebrows, with a look that said, 'some people are never satisfied'. I said to him, 'Socrates, why don't you tell Aristarchus the story of the dog?'

Socrates nodded and said, 'Excellent idea, Xenophon, but why don't you tell it, instead?'

So I told this fable, which Socrates had told me a few weeks before:

Long ago, when animals had the ability to speak, the sheep said to their owner, 'I don't understand you. You give nothing to us who supply you with lambs, wool, and cheese; while to your dog, who supplies you with nothing useful, you share the very food from your table.'

The dog, being told of these remarks, went to the sheep and told them, 'There is a very good reason why I share the food from the owner's table; for I'm the one who protects you, so that you are not stolen by thieves, or eaten by wolves. If I didn't guard you, you would be unable to even feed from the earth, for fear that you would be destroyed.'

Hearing this argument, the sheep agreed that the dog really did earn his privileges.'

'So you, Aristarchus, must tell your relatives that you, like the dog, are their guardian and protector, and that, by your means, they work and live in security and happiness, without suffering injury from anyone.'

I turned to Socrates. 'Am I right?'

'That's it, General, that's it exactly.'

Aristarchus thanked us both, and went off rehearsing the story to himself so that he wouldn't forget it by the time he got home.

12

THE LETTER

*In Which Xenophon Decides
to Leave Athens and Socrates*

My friend Proxenus sent me a letter from Persia. He had joined the court of Cyrus, the brother of the King of Persia, and was thriving under his command. Would I be interested in joining them? It was an enticing offer. Cyrus had a tremendous reputation, and was a great leader of men. To be able to meet him and witness his court at first hand would be a great opportunity. I wanted to go, but was it right?

I decided to consult Socrates on whether I should make the journey.

Socrates was alarmed. He said that Cyrus had zealously supported Sparta in the war against Athens and would be considered an enemy of Athens. It would look bad for me to serve a possible enemy of the state. However, I expressed a strong desire to go. I was not getting younger, and I had nothing to show for my life to date. I needed to do something.

Socrates suggested I travel to Delphi and consult the oracle of Apollo. I made the journey and asked the oracle which gods I should sacrifice and pray to in order to most successfully and honourably perform my journey and to return in safety. The oracle gave me the answer that the god I should sacrifice and pray to was Jupiter the King.

When I returned to Athens and told Socrates what the oracle had said he was annoyed.

'You asked the wrong question! Why didn't you ask the oracle if you should go or stay at home? That's what you wanted to know.'

I decided to tell him the truth. 'I suppose I asked that question because I really want to make the trip. There's nothing for me here.'

'I see.'

'Will you give me your approval?'

'First, tell me if you bothered to look at that writing carved on the temple wall? Remember we spoke about it in the early days?'

'I remember very well. My first lesson: KNOW YOURSELF.'

'And do you now know yourself, General?'

'Better than when I first met you, Socrates, thanks to you. The inscription means that you must know who you are in order to live properly.'

'That's right, but to know who you really are is not easy. To know who you are, you must know what it is that you want, and what you believe in. You must know your own character, for as I keep telling you, your character forms your destiny. What is it that you want from this trip, General?'

'Proxenus tells me that Cyrus is one of the great men of our generation, and I would like to go and meet him, and see for myself.'

'And besides meeting this great leader, what do you hope to gain from the trip?'

'Cyrus helps and aids his friends, and he has rewarded Proxenus with land and wealth.'

'And is that what you hope for, that Cyrus will give you land and money?'

'He would only give me those things if I was worthy of them, and did him some service.'

'And what service do you think you could give him, that he doesn't already have?'

'I don't know.'

'Will you advise him on virtue?'

'If he asks me to advise him.'

'What if he doesn't listen to his advisor? Will you go or stay?'

'I suppose I would have to leave.'

He took this in. 'I can see the attraction for you, General. You're young and you want action and experience. Cyrus can provide it.'

I had a further thought. 'If Cyrus is as impressive as Proxenus says, he might provide me with a good subject for a history book, just as Thucydides has written about the war.'

'You're no Thucydides, General, but you do have the makings of a fine commander. I give you my blessing, because it's clear that you are going anyway, with or without it.'

I couldn't hold back a smile.

'You have a long sea journey to get to Cyrus. You could do worse than use the time to think about what it is you really want from life, General, and what you really believe.'

'I will do that, Socrates, and when I return I will tell you what I have discovered.'

'I'm an old man, General, I might not be around when you get back.'

'I have no worries on that score, Socrates. You're as strong as a bull and you'll outlive us all.'

But that was to be the last time I saw him. Had I known that this was to be our final parting, I would have stayed and talked, reminisced about the years that we had spent together, and thanked him for all of his care and friendship. He would have liked that, and I, I must admit that I would have liked it too.

Just another regret. But a young man with ambitions does not hang around out of sentiment, for time is fleeting. I said my goodbyes, hugged and kissed him, and turned away.

Part Three

THE VERDICT

Selections from Plato's Dialogues:
The Apology, Crito, Phaedo *(part)*

A NOTE ON
THE TEXT

I have used Benjamin Jowett's translations of Plato as the basis for my versions of the *Apology* (The Trial), *Crito* (Socrates in Prison) and the fragment of the *Phaedo* (Now The Hour of Sunset Was Near). These two and a bit dialogues represent the final thirty days of Socrates' life, from his trial to his death.

Plato is mentioned in the *Apology* as having attended the trial, and it is said in the *Phaedo* that he was too ill to attend the death of his friend and mentor. It's safe to assume that Plato was a regular visitor to Socrates in prison during the thirty days of his incarceration, so these two dialogues – *Apology* and *Crito* – are ones that have a solid historical basis.

Professor Gregory Vlastos and others consider the *Apology* as the first of Plato's works, and the *Crito* is also an early dialogue. Consequently, scholars generally agree that in these works Plato was trying to capture the character and thoughts of Socrates, without adding his own philosophical ideas, as he did in the later dialogues. My argument as detailed in Part One is that the *Phaedo* is a later dialogue which has Socrates expressing ideas on the soul which are in fact Plato's alone.

Xenophon also wrote an account of Socrates' trial, and I have used the beginning of his account, the pre-trial meeting between Socrates and Hermogenes, as the introduction to the trial.

THE TRIAL

Plato's Apology

Introduction

While waiting for the trial date to be set, Socrates' friends noticed that he was living exactly as he did before the indictment. He wandered through Athens, finding people to talk to, and he conversed on the usual subjects. He seemed completely unconcerned with the impending trial.

Hermogenes took him aside one day and told Socrates that his friends were concerned about whether he was preparing his defence. Socrates said, 'Don't you think, Hermogenes, that my whole life has been a preparation for this defence?'

Hermogenes didn't understand him, and asked what he meant by that. Socrates went on to say, 'I have spent my entire life, Hermogenes, trying not to do anything unjust. I take this to be the best preparation possible.'

Hermogenes became anxious. 'But Socrates,' he pleaded 'don't you know that the judges here in Athens are so influenced by the power of oratory that from a speech alone they can unjustly condemn a man to death, or acquit the guilty.'

'Of course I know this, and twice I have tried to sit down and compose a defence speech, but my inner spirit, that stubborn divine sign of mine, always opposes me.'

This news was not good; in fact it was disastrous. 'But Socrates, unless you defend yourself in court, they will find you guilty. You need to convince them and plead with them for your life.'

'Hermogenes, I will make a speech, but I won't plead for my life. I am innocent of these charges and my entire life is my defence. If that is not sufficient to convince them, then I understand that I may have to die.'

Hermogenes was shocked by this. 'Socrates, this isn't the right way to go about it. Let us find a skilled advocate to defend you.'

'No, Hermogenes, it's important that I speak for myself. I can't hide behind someone else. Anyway, I'm an old man, and maybe the gods think that this is the right time for me to die.'

'Don't talk like this. You're still healthy and strong. You could go on for years.'

'Hermogenes, I have lived my life correctly and happily; I have done my duty both to the gods and to mankind. But if I am now spared, and my life prolonged, what can stop the infirmities of old age falling on me. My sight will grow dim, my hearing fade. Less able to learn new things and more likely to forget what I already know, I will become sadly aware of my decay, and the happiness that I felt all my life will wither away. This is not a happy ending.'

'Neither is being condemned by the state.'

'I agree, but I will give the judges my opinion of myself, and declare what I think I have deserved of gods and men, and if they are displeased with me, then I would rather submit to their judgement than prolong my life through tears and pleading.'

The Trial

ATHENS, 399 B.C.E.
THE LAW COURTS
The trial took place in the open air Law Courts and lasted for the customary one day. There were three accusers: Meletus, Anytus, and Lycon who spoke first, and their accusations

were that Socrates ignored the gods that the state recognised, introduced new gods of his own devising, and corrupted the young of Athens.

After the accusers stated the charges against Socrates the seventy-year-old philosopher rose to address the jury of five hundred citizens:

SOCRATES: Athenians, I don't know how you reacted to the speeches of my accusers, but I found the force of their eloquence to be so strong that their arguments nearly swept me off my feet, and I almost forgot my own name.

Even so, they have barely spoken a word of truth.

Among their many lies was one that really amazed me – when they told you to be careful, and not to let yourselves be deceived by the force of my eloquence. They should be ashamed of having said this, because they were sure to be shown up as soon as I opened my mouth and displayed my ineptitude as a speaker, unless by the force of eloquence they mean the force of truth; for there I do admit I am eloquent, but in a completely different way than theirs!

My accusers have hardly said a word of truth; but from me you shall hear the whole truth: not delivered, like theirs, as an elaborate oration decorated with fine words and phrases. No, I shall use only the words and arguments that occur to me as I speak; I am certain this is the right approach. At my time of life, to appear in front of you in the character of a junior orator, making florid speeches, would be ridiculous. Let no one expect this of me.

However, I do have one favour to ask. If you hear me using the same language in my defence which I have always been in the habit of using – and which many of you have heard, in the marketplace, and at the tables of the money-changers, for example – do not be surprised, and do not interrupt. Although I am over seventy years old, this is my first appearance in a court of law, and so I am a complete stranger to the ways of the place. Therefore, I would like you to regard me as if I really were a foreigner, whom you would naturally excuse if he spoke in his native tongue. This is not an unfair request. Never mind the manner of my speech, which may or may not be good, but think only of the justice of my cause, and concentrate on that. It is the duty of the judges to decide justly and for those who speak to utter only the truth.

The Early Slanders

My opponents, and the charges against me, are of two kinds – one recent, the other much older. First, I would like to reply to the earliest charges and to my first accusers, and then I will move on to the ones you heard today. I make this distinction because I have had many accusers over the years, and their false charges have haunted me for a very long time. I am really more afraid of these old slanders than I am of Meletus and his associates, who, although formidable in their own way, are not as dangerous as the old accusers.

When you were children, they tried to take possession of your minds with lies about an eccentric called Socrates, a Sophist, who speculated about the heavens above, and the earth below, and who could make the poorer argument seem like the better one.

These are the accusers I fear the most, because they spread these malicious rumours for years, and those who heard them were all too ready to imagine that anyone who speculates about such strange things must be an atheist. When you heard these rumours you may have been at an impressionable age and there was no one to explain them away or to defend me. And, worst of all, I do not even know the names of these anonymous slanderers, who from envy and malice have stirred you up. They are the most difficult to deal with, since I cannot bring them here to question, and therefore I must simply fight with shadows in my own defence, and question when there is no one to answer.

But I know I must begin my defence, and I will try, in the short time allowed, to do away with this poor opinion of me which you have held for such a long time. I hope I can succeed, and that my words find favour with you, but I know that to accomplish this will not be easy – I am well aware of the difficulty of my task. However, let the outcome be as God wills: in obedience to the law I make my defence.

I will begin at the beginning, and ask what the accusation is that has given rise to these slanders against me, and has encouraged Meletus to issue today's proceedings. What do these slanderers say in attacking me? *They* are really my prosecutors, and I will sum up their charge:

'Socrates is an evil-doer, and a strange person, who searches into things in heaven and in earth, and who makes the weaker argument defeat the stronger; and he teaches these harmful things to others.'

That is the nature of the accusation, and you may have seen something similar for yourselves in a comedy by Aristophanes, called *Clouds*. Aristophanes introduces a man whom he calls Socrates, going around saying that he can walk on air, and talking a load of nonsense about matters that I don't pretend to know anything about. Not that I want to disparage anyone who studies natural philosophy. I should be very sorry if Meletus could charge me with that – but the simple truth is, I have nothing to do with these kinds of studies. A great number of people here today are witnesses to the truth of this, and I appeal to them to speak up. Many of you have heard me speak, and I would like you to tell your neighbours if any of you have ever heard me talking on matters of this kind . . .

(Socrates' supporters and friends confirm this to the assembly.)

You hear their answer. And from this you can understand that the other slanders against me are equally false.

I Am Not a Teacher

There is just as little foundation for the rumour that I am a teacher, and charge fees; that is no more true than the other. If someone is qualified to teach, I respect him for being paid, like Gorgias of Leontium, and Prodicus of Ceos, and Hippias of Elis. They travel around all the cities and persuade young men to leave their own homes, where they could be taught for free, and to join them, whom they not only pay, but are actually grateful for the chance to do so.

I recently heard of such a philosopher visiting Athens: I know a man who has spent an enormous sum of money on the Sophists – Callias the son of Hipponicus – and knowing that he has sons, I asked him:

'Callias, if your two sons were foals or calves, there would be no difficulty in finding someone to look after them; you would probably hire a trainer of horses or a farmer who could improve and perfect their appropriate nature. But, seeing as they are human beings, whom do you think should instruct them? Is there an expert who perfects human qualities? I assume you've thought about this – is there someone like this?'

'There is,' he said.

'Who is he,' I said, 'and what does he charge?'

'Evenus the Parian is the man, and his fee is five minae.'

'Well, lucky Evenus!' I said to myself, 'To have such wonderful wisdom, and to teach it for such a modest fee.'

If I had such wisdom, I would no doubt become very proud and conceited; but the truth is that I do not have any knowledge of this kind.

I imagine some of you might say:

'Why is this, Socrates? What is the origin of these accusations against you? You must have been doing something strange, because all this infamy and rumour about you would never have arisen if you had been like other men. Tell us the reason so we are not forced to invent it for ourselves.'

That is a good question, and I will try to explain to you the origin of this term 'wise', and of my poor reputation. Please listen, for although some of you may think I am joking, I assure you that I will tell you the entire truth.

Athenians, this reputation of mine has come about because of a certain kind of wisdom I possess. What kind of wisdom is this? It's a very human wisdom of the kind anyone can acquire, and in this extremely limited sense I think I am wise. The 'geniuses' I spoke of before have a superhuman wisdom, which I cannot describe, since I do not possess it myself; and anyone who says that I have is lying and distorting my character.

(There are interruptions from the assembly)

I would like to remind you not to interrupt me, even if I am going to say something that seems outrageous. For the words that I am next going to speak are not mine. I would now like to call my first witness, one who is extremely worthy of your belief, and who will tell you about my wisdom – whether I have any, and of what sort – and that witness is – the god of Delphi . . .

(There are surprised responses from the assembly)

The Oracle

You must have known the late Chaerephon; he was one of my oldest friends, and also a good democrat who took part in the recent exile and return of the people. Well, Chaerephon, as you know, was very impetuous in everything he did, and once he actually travelled to Delphi to boldly ask the oracle to tell him whether – as I was saying, I must beg you not to interrupt – he asked whether there was anyone wiser than Socrates, and the oracle answered that there was no one. Chaerephon's brother, who is in court, can confirm the truth of this story.

Why do I mention this? Because I am going to explain to you how the attack on my reputation began. When Chaerephon told me the oracle's answer, I said to myself, 'What can the god mean? What is the interpretation of this riddle? I know that I have no real wisdom, small or great, so what can he mean when he says that I am the wisest of men? He can't be lying, because he is a god; that would be against his nature.'

My Mission

After contemplating the riddle for quite some time, I finally thought of a way to test its truth. I thought that if I could only find a man wiser than myself, then I could go back to the god with a clear refutation. I would say to the god, 'You said that I was the wisest man, but here is a person wiser than me.'

At the time of this experience, I was studying one of our famous politicians, Pericles, so I decided to start with him. When I began to question him, I could not help thinking that he was not really so wise, although many people thought he was, and Pericles himself thought he was extremely wise. I tried to explain to him that he thought he was wise, but that he really wasn't. Well, he didn't like to hear this, and the upshot was that he hated me, and his enmity was shared by all his friends who heard our conversation. So I left him, saying to myself, as I went away, 'Well, although I don't suppose either of us has any real knowledge to boast of, I am better off than he – for he knows nothing, but thinks that he does, whereas I am certain that I know nothing.'

In this way, it seemed I had a slight advantage over him, since at least I didn't think I knew what I really did not know.

So I went to a second man, Protagoras, who had still higher philosophical pretensions, and my conclusion was exactly the same. And I made another enemy of him, and of many more besides.

Following this I questioned one man after another, always conscious of the anger and hatred that I provoked, which distressed and alarmed me. But necessity drove me on – the word of God, I thought, must be considered first. So I said to myself, you must visit *everyone* who appears to know something, and discover the true meaning of the oracle. And I swear to you, fellow citizens, I swear! – for I must tell you the truth – the result of my mission was just this: I found that the men with the greatest reputation were almost always the most foolish; and some with no status at all were really wiser and better.

I will tell you the tale of my wanderings and of the 'Herculean labours', as I call them, which I endured, only to find at last that the oracle was correct. When I left the politicians, I went to the poets: dramatic, lyric, and all sorts. Now here, I said to myself, you will be shown up; you will find out that compared to them you are an ignoramus.

Accordingly, I took them some of the best of their own writings, and asked about the meaning of them – thinking they would teach me something. I am almost ashamed to say this, but I have to confess that there is hardly a person here who would not have explained their poetry better than they did themselves. That showed me immediately that poets do not write poetry by wisdom, but by a sort of genius or inspiration. They are like diviners or soothsayers, who also say many fine things but don't understand the meaning of them. I also saw that on the strength of their poetry they believed themselves to be the wisest of men in other things in which they were in fact totally ignorant. So I left, considering myself superior to them for the same reason that I was superior to the politicians.

Finally, I went to the skilled craftsmen, for I was sure they knew many fine things. In this I was not mistaken, for they did know many things of which I was ignorant, and in this they were certainly wiser than I.

But I observed that even the craftsmen fell into the same error as the poets; because they were good artisans, they thought they also knew all sorts of other lofty matters, and this error in them overshadowed their wisdom. So I asked myself on behalf of the oracle whether I would prefer to be as I was – without having their knowledge *or* their ignorance, or to be like them in both; and I answered myself and the oracle that I was better off as I was.

These investigations of mine have generated a great deal of hostility and resentment against me, as you can well imagine, and have had the unfortunate consequence of people calling me wise, because my listeners always assumed that I possessed the wisdom I could not find in others.

His Conclusion

The real truth, Athenians, is that only God is wise; and by this oracle he wants to tell us that human wisdom is something completely insignificant. He is not speaking literally of Socrates, but is only using my name as an illustration, as if he were to say to us, 'The wisest of you mortals is one who, like Socrates, knows that his wisdom is in truth worth nothing.'

And so I go on my way, obedient to this divine command, and I question the wisdom of anyone, citizen or foreigner, who appears to be wise; if he is not wise, then in vindication of the oracle I must show him that he is not. This occupation so absorbs me that I have no time for either public matters or my own concerns. In fact, my devotion to god's command has reduced me and my family to utter poverty.

His Followers

There is one other reason for my unpopularity. Young men of the upper classes, who have time to spare, have gathered around me of their own accord. They like to hear me question other people, and often imitate me, trying to question others themselves. They soon enough discover there are plenty of people who think they know something, but really know little or nothing. Those they question, instead of becoming angry with themselves for being foolish, become angry with me.

'This wretched Socrates!' they say, 'this perverse and wrong-headed teacher of youth!'

And then if somebody asks them, 'Why, what evil does he practise or teach?' they don't know, and can't answer; but since they don't want to look stupid, they repeat the clichés that are always thrown at philosophers about teaching things beyond the clouds and beneath the earth, and being an atheist, and making the poorer argument defeat the better one. They don't like to confess that their pretending to knowledge has been detected, which is really the truth.

Many of these people are ambitious and energetic, are combative and have persuasive tongues, and they have carefully worked out a very plausible case against me. In guarding their own reputations they have filled your ears with violent denunciations of me. This is the reason why my three accusers, Meletus, Anytus and Lycon, have attacked me; Meletus on behalf of the poets, Anytus on behalf of the craftsmen, and Lycon, on behalf of the rhetoricians. As I said before, I can't expect to get rid of this cluster of libels in such a short time.

This, my fellow citizens, is the truth and the whole truth. I have not concealed anything and I have not spoken falsely. But I know that it is this direct speaking of mine that makes them hate me, and this is proof that I am speaking the truth – this is the cause and reason of the slanders against me. If you inquire into them now or later, you will find the facts to be just as I have described them.

The New Accusers

I have said enough in my defence about the earlier accusers; I shall now defend myself against the more recent ones, who are headed by Meletus, that principled and patriotic man, as he calls himself. And then I will try to defend myself against the rest.

These new accusers also deserve to have their charges read. What do they say? Something like this: that Socrates is guilty of corrupting the minds of the young, not believing in the gods of the state, and introducing new deities of his own making. Those are the charges. Let's examine them, one by one.

Corrupting the Young

First, Meletus says that I practise evil by corrupting the young. But I think that Meletus is the real evil-doer, because he makes a joke of a serious matter, since he brings people to trial on frivolous grounds from a pretended fervour and interest in matters about which he really doesn't care in the slightest. I will try to prove the truth of this to your satisfaction.

Meletus, come over here and let me ask you a question. Do you often think about the improvement of the young?

'Yes, I do.'

Tell the judges, then, who has a good influence on the young. Obviously you must know, since you have taken so much trouble to discover who corrupts them, and are citing and accusing me in front of the judges. Please tell them who is a good influence on the young.

You are silent, Meletus, and have no answer. Isn't this rather disgraceful, and a very strong proof of what I said, that you have absolutely no interest in the matter? Come on, speak up, and tell us who improves the young?

'The laws.'

That's not what I meant, and you know it. I want you to name who the *person* is whose concern it is to know the laws.

'The members of the jury, Socrates, who are here today.'

Do you mean to say, Meletus, that the jurors are able to educate and improve the young?

'Certainly they are.'

What, all of them, or only some?

'All of them.'

Well, what good news! So many benefactors! And what about the audience, do they improve them?

'Yes, they do.'

And the senators?

'Yes, the senators, too.'

Perhaps the members of the Assembly corrupt them? Or are they also improvers?

'They also improve them.'

So it seems that every Athenian improves and aids the young, with the sole exception of myself; and I alone am their corrupter. Is that what you really affirm?

'Most emphatically.'

This is certainly an unfortunate quality you have detected in me. Suppose I ask you another question.

Is this also true in the case of horses? Does one man do them harm and all the rest of the world do them good? Or isn't the exact opposite of this true, that only a few people – horse trainers – are able to do them good, while others who use horses injure them somewhat? Isn't that true, Meletus, of horses, and all other animals?

Yes, of course it is, whether you answer or not. The young would be very pleased if they had only one corrupter, with everyone else their improvers. I have no more to add. This is ample proof, Meletus, that you have never had a single thought about the young: you make it clear that you do not have the least care or interest in the cause that has led you to accuse me.

Now, Meletus, don't go away, I want to ask you another question. Which is better, to live among bad citizens, or among good ones? Come on, Meletus, answer the question, it's not that difficult. Is it true that good citizens do their neighbours good, and bad ones have a bad effect?

'Certainly.'

And is there anyone who would rather be harmed than benefited by those who live with him? Answer, please, Meletus, the law demands that you answer. Does anyone prefer to be injured?

'Certainly not.'

Now when you accuse me of corrupting and debasing the young, do you allege that I do so intentionally or unintentionally?

'Intentionally of course.'

You have just admitted that good citizens do their neighbours good, and bad ones do them harm. Now, is that a truth which your superior wisdom has recognised so early in life, and I, in my senility, am in such woeful ignorance as not to know that if I corrupt a man with whom I have to live, I am very likely to be harmed by him? Yet, knowing this, I still go ahead and corrupt him, and intentionally, too? That is what you are saying, Meletus, and I for one do not believe it and don't think any other sane person would, either.

I believe that either I am a good influence on the young, or I corrupt them unintentionally, so in either case your accusation is false. If my offence is unintentional, I should not have been summoned to this court. You should have taken me aside privately, to warn and counsel me; because if you had advised me, I would surely have stopped doing something that I did not intend to do. But you refused to approach me and enlighten me, but instead you indicted me in this court, which is a place not of instruction, but of punishment.

Belief in the Gods

It is quite clear by now that Meletus has no interest at all, great or small, in this matter. But still I would like to know, Meletus, how it is alleged that I corrupt the minds of the young. I suppose you mean, in terms of your indictment, that I teach them to acknowledge new divinities or spiritual agencies instead of the gods which the state recognises. Are these the lessons which deprave the young?

'Yes, they are.'

Then, in the name of the gods that we are discussing, Meletus, tell me and the court, in plain language, what it is you mean! I do not understand whether you assert that I teach others to acknowledge some gods – which implies that I believe in them and am not a complete atheist, so I can't be guilty of that – or that they are not the same gods which the city recognises, so that the charge is that they are different gods. Or, do you really mean to say that I am simply an atheist, and a teacher of atheism?

'I mean just that – you are a complete atheist.'

That is an extraordinary thing to say, Meletus! What is your object in saying that? Do you mean that I do not believe in the sun and moon as gods, which is the common belief of everyone?

'I assure you, judges, he does not believe in them, because he says that the Sun is a stone, and the Moon a chunk of Earth.'

Dear Meletus, you must be imagining that you are prosecuting the old philosopher Anaxagoras. You must have a very low opinion of our judges if you believe them so ignorant as not to know that the books of Anaxagoras are full of those silly doctrines. And do you seriously consider that these are the doctrines that the young are said to learn from Socrates, when they can buy these books in the market for a drachma at the most, and so laugh at me if I were to pretend to have originated such eccentric ideas.

Meletus, do you honestly think that I do not believe in any god?

'I swear by Zeus that you believe in absolutely none at all.'

You are basically a liar, Meletus, and I suspect that you don't even believe yourself. I can't help thinking, fellow citizens, that Meletus is a reckless bully, and that he's brought this indictment in a spirit of wanton aggression and youthful bravado. You know, I suspect he has devised a clever riddle, wanting to test my intelligence. He said to himself, 'I shall find out whether this wise old bird will discover how I have ingeniously contradicted myself for my own amusement, or whether I can deceive him and the rest of them!' Because

Meletus certainly does appear to me to contradict himself in the indictment; it is as if he said: Socrates is not only guilty of not believing in the gods, but he is also guilty of believing in them too – surely this must be a joke.

I would like you, Athenians, to join me in examining the line of reasoning which leads me to this conclusion. You, Meletus, must answer me. And I must remind you, as I requested, that you are not to interrupt me if I speak in my normal way.

Is there anyone, Meletus, who believes in the existence of human activities, but not in the existence of human beings? ... I wish, fellow citizens, that he would answer, and not make these continual interruptions. Is there anyone who believes in horsemanship, but not in horses? Or in flute-playing, but not in flute-players?

Since you refuse to answer for yourself I'll answer for you. No, my worthy friend, there is no one who ever did. Now, please, answer the next question. Is there anyone who believes in spiritual and divine powers, and not in spirits or supernatural beings?

'No.'

I'm so pleased to have extracted such a full answer, with the aid of the court; nevertheless, you swear in the indictment that I teach and believe in divine or spiritual agencies. Now it doesn't matter whether these are new or old, because I *do* happen to believe in spiritual powers, which you swear in your affidavit. But if I believe in divine powers, I must also believe in spirits or supernatural beings. Isn't that obviously true? ... Yes, it is true, since your silence testifies to that. Now what are spirits or supernatural beings? Aren't they either gods or the children of gods? Is that true?

'Yes, that is true.'

Thank you, Meletus. Now here is that ingenious riddle that I mentioned: first you claim that I don't believe in gods, and later you state that I do believe in them. If supernatural beings or spirits are gods as you have agreed, then I must believe in gods since I believe in supernatural beings. Because, if supernatural beings are the illegitimate children of gods, as everyone believes, this necessarily implies the existence of their parents. You might as well assert the existence of foals and colts, and deny that of horses. This nonsense, Meletus, could only have been intended by you as some weird intelligence test, or more likely you put this into the indictment because you actually had nothing real to accuse me of. No one with a glimmer of understanding will ever be convinced that the same man can believe in divine and superhuman things, yet not believe that there are gods and supernatural beings.

I don't think I need to defend myself further against Meletus' flimsy accusation. But it shows that I certainly have many enemies, and this is what will cause my destruction if anything does – not Meletus or Anytus – but the envy and derision of a great many people, which has been the death of many innocent men, and will probably be the death of many more; there is no likelihood of my being the last.

His Way of Life

Someone might say: 'Aren't you ashamed, Socrates, to live a way of life which is likely to bring you to an untimely end?'

To that question I would reply, There you are mistaken – a person who is good for anything at all should not calculate the chances of living or dying; he only needs to consider whether in doing anything he is doing right or wrong, acting the part of a good person or of a bad one. According to your view, the heroes who fell at Troy were not good for much, and Achilles above all, who disregarded danger in comparison with disgrace. When his goddess mother warned him, eager as he was to slay Hector, that if he avenged his companion Patroclus by killing Hector, he would then die himself – 'Fate,' she said, 'waits for you next after Hector' – Achilles, hearing this, discounted danger and death, and feared instead to live in dishonour, and failing to avenge his friend. 'Let me avenge my enemy,' he replied, 'and die now, rather than squat here to be mocked, a burden on the earth.' Did Achilles have any concern about death and danger?

For wherever a man's place is, whether it's one he has chosen or one in which he has been placed by a commander, I believe that there he must remain even in the hour of danger, taking no account of death or of anything else, but only of his possible disgrace. And this, my fellow citizens, is as true a saying as I know.

It would be ridiculous if I, who, when ordered by the generals whom you chose to command me at Potidaea and Amphipolis and Delium, remained just where they placed me, like every other man, facing possible death; and now if I, when God orders me to fulfil the philosopher's mission of searching into myself and others, were to desert my post through fear of death, or any other danger. That would indeed be strange, and I would justly be brought to court for denying the existence of the gods, if I disobeyed the oracle because of fear of death, and for imagining I am wise when I am not. Because the fear of death is the same as the pretence of wisdom, since it represents the appearance of knowing the unknown. No one knows whether death, which people through fear consider the greatest evil, may not really be the greatest blessing. Isn't that a supposition of knowledge, which is the worst kind of ignorance?

And this is where, I think, I have an advantage over the rest of mankind, and if I were to claim that I were wiser than other men it would only be in this: that since I know very little about the afterlife, I don't suppose that I do know. But what I *do* know is that disobedience to my superior, whether God or a person, is evil and dishonorable, and I will never fear or avoid something which may be a blessing rather than a certain evil.

If you free me now, and reject the suggestion of Anytus, who said that if I am not exterminated I should never have been prosecuted, but that if I escape death, your sons will all be utterly ruined by listening to my words; so if you now say to me, 'Socrates, this time we will not listen to Anytus, and will let you off, but with one condition, that you must abandon your quest and stop questioning in this way any more, and if you are caught doing this again you will die,' if this was the condition on which you would release me, I would reply, 'Athenians, I honour and love you; but I must obey God rather than you, and while I have life and strength I shall never cease from the practice of philosophy, advising and searching for the truth from everyone I meet.'

I shall go on saying, in my usual way, 'My friend, why do you, a citizen of the greatest and most famous city of the world for its wisdom, care so much about accumulating the greatest amount of money, glory and status, and so little of wisdom, truth and the improvement of your soul, which you never pay the slightest attention to? Aren't you ashamed of this?'

If someone claims to care about his soul, I do not abandon him or let him go, but interrogate and examine and cross-examine him, and if I think he has no virtue, but only says that he has, I criticise him for neglecting what is of prime importance, and giving all his attention to trivialities.

And this is what I say to everyone I meet, young and old, citizen and stranger, but especially to the citizens, since they are my brothers. For this is the command of God, as I told you, and I believe that no greater blessing has ever happened to Athens than my service to God. Because my only occupation is to go around persuading you all, young and old, to make your chief concern not your bodies or your possessions, but to care only for the most radical improvement of your souls. I will never stop telling you that wealth does not bring goodness, but instead it is from goodness that wealth and every other blessing comes both to the individual and to the state. This is my message, and if this is the doctrine that corrupts the young, then my influence must indeed be truly harmful.

If anyone denies that this is my teaching, he is a complete liar. The choice is yours, Athenians, either acquit me or condemn me; but whatever you do, you must know that I shall never alter my ways, even if I have to die a thousand times.

(There are shouts from the Assembly)

The Horsefly

Athenians, please do not interrupt – there was an agreement between us that you should hear me out. And I think that what I am about to say to you will do you some good: for I have something more to say, which you may also want to shout about; but I ask you to restrain yourselves. I want you to be aware that if you kill someone like me, you will injure yourselves much more than you will injure me. Meletus and Anytus will not injure me: they don't have the power, because I do not believe that the law of God permits a better man to be harmed by a worse. I do not deny that a bad man may put a good man to death, or drive him into exile, or deprive him of his civil rights. They and others may imagine that these are great evils, but I do not agree with them. I believe that to do what Anytus is doing – trying to take away an inno-cent man's life – is a far greater evil.

And now, Athenians, I am not going to argue for my own sake, as you might expect, but for yours, that you may not sin against God, or lightly reject his gift by condemning me. For if you kill me you will not easily find another like me who, if I may use such a ludicrous expression, is a sort of gadfly, given to the state by God; the state is like a thor-oughbred stallion who is sluggish owing to his great size, and needs to be stirred into life. It seems to me that I am the gadfly which God has given the state, and all day long and in all places I am always landing on you, arousing and persuading and reproaching you. And as you will not easily find another like me, I advise you to spare my life. I understand that you feel irritated at being suddenly awakened from your nap, and in your annoyance you may take Anytus's advice and finish me off with a single slap, which you easily might, and then will go on sleeping for the remainder of your lives, unless God in his care for you gives you another gadfly to take my place. That God has given me to you is proved by this – if I had been like other men, I would not have neglected my own concerns, or patiently seen them neglected during all these years, but I have busied myself all the time on your behalf, coming to you individually, like a father or elder brother, admonishing you to regard virtue. This is not like human nature.

If I had gained anything, or had been paid for my advice, there would have been some sense in my conduct. But, as you can see, not even the impudence of my accusers dares to say that I have ever exacted or sought pay from anyone. The witness I have to prove the truth of this is a convincing one – it is my poverty.

Why He Avoids Politics

Some of you have wondered why I go around in private, giving advice and busying myself with the concerns of others, but have not ventured to come forward in public and advise the state. I will give you the reason for this.

You have often heard me talk of the oracle that speaks to me, and is the sign or spirit or divinity that Meletus ridicules in the indictment. This sign has been with me ever since I was a child. It is a voice which comes to me and always forbids me to do or say something I am planning on, but it never encourages me. This is what stands in the way of my being a politician. And rightly, as I think, because I am certain, Athenians, that if I had engaged in politics, I would have died long ago and done no good either to you or to myself. Please don't be offended if I tell you the truth:

the person who conscientiously opposes the will of the people, honestly struggling against illegalities and wrongs taking place, will not be able to preserve his life. The person who is a true champion of justice, if he wants to survive even for a short time, must combat injustice privately and leave politics alone.

As proof of this I will give you not just theories but what you value more – facts. Let me tell you about an incident from my own life, which will prove to you that I would never yield to injustice from fear of death, even at the cost of my own life. It's a commonplace story, of a kind that's often heard in these courts, but nevertheless it's true.

The only official position I ever held, Athenians, was that of a senator elected to the council; my group was acting as the Presidency during the trial of the nine generals who failed to rescue the men who were slain in the naval battle of Arginusae. The Assembly proposed to have a group trial, which was illegal. At the time I was the only one of the Presidents who insisted that you should not act unconstitutionally, and put my vote against the proposal. When the speakers threatened to impeach and arrest me, and you all shrieked at the top of your voices urging them on, I made up my mind that I would rather run the risk of imprisonment and death with law and justice on my side, than support you in your injustice because of fear.

This happened in the days of the democracy. Later, when the Thirty Tyrants were in power, they called me and four others into the rotunda, and ordered us to travel to Salamis, arrest Leon, and bring him back for execution. This was the kind of command they were always giving, wanting to implicate as many people as possible in their crimes. At this time again I showed, not only in words, but also in action, that – if I may be allowed to use such an expression – I cared not a straw for death, and my only fear was the fear of doing an unrighteous or an unholy act.

For as powerful as that oppressive tyranny was it did not

frighten me into doing wrong. When we left the rotunda the other four men went as ordered to Salamis to bring Leon to Athens to be killed, but I, I turned away and walked quietly home. For this act I might have lost my life, had the power of the Tyrants not shortly afterwards come to an end. And many people can be witnesses to this.

Can you really imagine my surviving into old age if I had led a public life, conducting myself like an honourable man in what was right, and making justice, as I should, the most important thing?

No, indeed, Athenians, neither I nor any other man would have lived long. But I have always been consistent in all my actions, public as well as private. I have never approved any action incompatible with justice on the part of anyone, including those who are maliciously called my disciples. Because the truth is that I have never set myself up as a teacher, but if anyone wants to come and hear me while I am pursuing my mission, whether young or old, they can freely come. I do not charge a fee for talking; but anyone, rich or poor, can question and answer me and listen to my words. Whether he turns out to be a bad citizen or a good one, that you cannot blame me for, since I never imparted any teaching to anyone. If anyone claims that he has learned or heard anything from me in private which no one else has heard, you can be sure that he is speaking falsely.

Not a Corrupter of the Young

You may ask me, 'Socrates, why do people delight in continually conversing with you?'

I have already told you, Athenians, the whole truth about this: they like to hear my cross-examination of the pretenders to wisdom; this can sometimes be amusing. And this is a duty which the God has imposed on me, and I have been assured of this by oracles, visions, and every other way that the will of divine power signifies to us. This is true, Athenians – if it were not, it would soon be refuted.

If I have really corrupted the young, those who have grown up and are now aware that I gave them bad advice would come forward as accusers to denounce me. If they did not want to come themselves, you would expect some of their relatives, fathers, or brothers, to say what harm their families suffered at my hands. Now is their time. Many of them are here in court. There is Crito, my contemporary and neighbour; and there is Critobulus his son. There is Lysanias of Sphettus, who is the father of Aeschines; and there is Antiphon of Cephisus, who is the father of Epigenes. There are also many brothers of men who have associated with me. There is Nicostratus the son of Theosdotides, and the brother of Theodotus; and there is Paralus the son of Demodocus, whose brother was Theages; and Adeimantus the son of Ariston, whose brother Plato is present; and Aeantodorus, who is the brother of Apollodorus, whom I also see. I could mention a great many others, any of whom Meletus could have produced as witnesses. If he forgot to do so, let him call them now. I am willing to make way for him. And let him state if he has any testimony to produce.

No, Athenians, the exact opposite is the truth. All of these men are ready to support me – the corrupter and evil genius of their relatives, as Meletus and Anytus call me. The corrupted youth might have a motive for that, but as for their uncorrupted elder relatives – why should they support me with their testimony? Why, indeed, except for the sake of truth and justice, and because they know that I am speaking the truth, and that Meletus is lying.

Final Plea

Well, Athenians, this is nearly all the defence I can offer. Just one more thing. Perhaps some of you may feel annoyed when you recall how you yourselves, standing trial on a less serious charge than mine, resorted to prayers and tears, and how you produced your tiny children in court, which made a very moving spectacle, together with a posse of your relations and friends; whereas I, who am probably in the utmost danger, will not do any of these things. Perhaps this may prejudice some of you against me, and make you vote in anger because you are affronted by this. If there are any like this among you, I would say to you: my friends, I am a man, and, like other men, am a creature of flesh and blood, not made of wood or stone, as Homer says; yes, I have a family, and three sons too, one of whom is grown up, and the other two still children; but I will not bring any of them here in order to beg you for an acquittal. Why not? Not from being pig-headed or indifferent to your power. Whether I am or am not afraid of death is another question, which I will not speak of now. The point is simply that I feel such conduct is discreditable to myself, to you, and to the whole state.

Someone as old as I am, who has a reputation for wisdom, whether deserved or not, should not debase himself like that. At any rate, the world has decided that Socrates is in some way different to other men. Now if those among you who are said to be superior in wisdom or courage demean yourselves in this way, how shameful is your conduct! I have seen men of reputation, when they have been brought to trial, behaving in the strangest manner. They seemed to imagine that it would be simply dreadful if they lost their lives – as though they would be immortal if you only allowed them to live! I think they brought disgrace to the city. Any stranger coming in would say of them that the most eminent men of Athens, to whom the Athenians themselves give respect and command, are no better than children. I say that these things should not to be done by those of us who are even slightly eminent; and if they are done, you should not permit it. Instead you should show that you are more inclined to condemn, not the person who is quiet, but the person who creates a pathetic scene, and brings ridicule on the city.

Setting aside the question of disgrace, there seems to be something wrong in imploring a judge, and so procuring an acquittal, instead of informing him of the facts and convincing him by argument. For the jury does not make a gift of justice, but decides where justice lies; and the jury has sworn to judge according to the laws, and not according to its own whim. None of us should get into the habit of perjuring ourselves – that would be sinful for us both. Therefore, you must not ask me to do what I consider disgraceful or impious or wrong, especially now, when I am being tried for impiety. For if, Athenians, I could persuade you to go against your solemn oath, then I would be teaching you contempt for religion, and so convict myself, in my own defence, of not having any religious beliefs.

But that is not the truth; I have a more profound belief in the gods than any of my accusers, and I leave it now to you and to God to judge me as it shall be best for us all.

(The jury's vote is counted and finds Socrates guilty, by a thirty-vote majority.)

Socrates' Proposal for his Sentence

There are many reasons why I am not dismayed, Athenians, at this guilty verdict. I had actually expected it, and I'm only surprised that the votes are nearly equal. I had thought that the majority against me would be far larger, but now, if thirty votes had gone over to the other side, I would have been acquitted. Even as it stands I feel that in regard to Meletus' accusations I have been acquitted. In fact, if Anytus and Lycon had not also accused me, he would not have had a fifth of the votes, and would have lost his thousand drachmas as the law states.

Meletus has proposed my death as the penalty. What shall I propose to you, Athenians? Obviously, it must be adequate. And what should I pay or suffer for what I have done? What shall be done to a man who has never had the sense to be idle during his whole life? Who has never cared about what everyone else cares about – wealth, family interests, and status, speaking in the assembly, being a magistrate, and secret plots and political parties?

Realising that I was too honest a man to follow in that way and live, I did not go where I could do no good to you or to myself. Instead, I set myself the task of doing the greatest good privately to everyone. I tried to persuade all of you that you must first look into yourselves, and cultivate virtue and wisdom before you look after your own private interests; and to look after the state itself before you look after its interests; and this should be the order to observe in all your actions.

What should be done with such a person? No doubt it should be something good, Athenians, if he is to have what he really deserves; and the benefit should be of a kind suitable to him. What would be an appropriate award for him? What would be an appropriate award for a poor man who is a public benefactor, who needs leisure time so that he can continue to encourage you? I think nothing can be more fitting for such a person than maintenance by the state for the rest of his life. This reward I deserve far more than a winner in the races at the Olympics. Because I am in need, whereas he has more than enough; and he only gives you the appearance of success, while I give you the reality. So if I am to estimate a penalty that accords with justice, I suggest that maintenance by the state is a reasonable return.

(The assembly responds badly to this suggestion)

You may think I am mocking you in saying this, in the same way as before when I spoke about those pathetic appeals. That is not the case. I say this because I am convinced that I never intentionally 'wrong' anyone, although I cannot convince you of this – because we have had so little time for discussion. If it was the custom in Athens, as it is in other cities, that a capital case should be heard over several days, then I believe I could have convinced you. But now the time is too short, and I cannot in an instant refute grave allegations; since I am convinced that I have never harmed anyone, I will certainly not wrong myself by asserting that I deserve punishment, or by proposing some kind of penalty. Why should I? Because I am afraid of the death penalty, when, as I said, I don't know whether death is a good or an evil? Do you expect me to propose a penalty which certainly would be an evil? Imprisonment? Why should I live in prison, and be the slave of the magistrates? Or should the penalty be a fine, and imprisonment until it is paid? Here I have the same objection, because I would have to languish in prison, lacking the money to pay the fine. And what if I say exile, which I suspect may be acceptable to you. I would have to be so desperately in love with life to think that if you, who are my fellow citizens, cannot endure my conversations any longer, and have found them so offensive and ugly that you desire no more of them, that others would be likely to tolerate them? No indeed, Athenians, that is not very likely. And what kind of life would I lead, at my age, wandering from city to city, living in ever-changing exile, and always being driven out! For I am quite sure that wherever I go, the young men will listen to my conversation, just as they do here. If I reject them, their elders will drive me out at the insistence of the young; and if I accept them, their fathers and friends will drive me out of their own accord for the sake of the young.

Someone may say, 'Yes, Socrates, but if you mind your own business, you can go into any foreign city, and no one will interfere with you?'

It has been very difficult for me to make you understand my answer to this. If I tell you that in obedience to a divine command, I cannot mind my own business, you will not believe that I am serious. If I tell you that to let no day pass without discussing goodness and other virtues, and to examine both myself and others, is really the very best thing that a person can do, and that a life which is unexamined is not worth living – *that* you are even less likely to believe. But that is really the way it is, Athenians, although it is very difficult for me to persuade you.

Besides, I am not used to thinking that I deserve punishment. If I had money I might have proposed to give you what I had, because that would not cause me any harm. But you see that I have none, and can only ask you to proportion the fine to my means. I think that I could afford one mina, and so propose a fine of that amount.

(He is interrupted by shouts)

... One moment please – Plato, Crito, Critobulus, and Apollodorus, my friends here, want me to propose thirty minae, and they will be the guarantors.

Alright then, say thirty minae, let that be the fine; and you can certainly rely on them to pay it.

(The jury votes again and condemns Socrates to death, with an increased majority of eighty votes.)

Socrates' Comments on his Sentence

Well, Athenians, for gaining a very small amount of time you are going to earn an evil reputation – and blame – from those who want to disparage the city, of having killed Socrates, 'that wise man' – because they will call me wise even though I am not, when they want to blame you. If you had waited a little while, your desire would have been fulfilled in the course of nature, since I am far advanced in years, and not far from death. I am speaking now only to those of you who voted to condemn me to death, and I have one final thing to say to you.

You think that I was convicted through lacking arguments that I could have used – I mean, that if I had decided to leave nothing undone, nothing unsaid, I might have received an acquittal. That is far from true; the deficiency which led to my conviction was not one of words – certainly not. It was a deficiency of audacity and impudence and inclination to address you as you would have liked me to – weeping, wailing and lamenting – and saying and doing many things which you usually hear from others, and which, as I have said, are unworthy of me. I thought that I should not do anything shabby or contemptible in the hour of danger, and I do not regret the handling of my defence. I would rather die, having spoken in my own way, than speak in your manner and live.

Neither in war nor at law should a person use every possible means to escape death. In battle it often happens that if a man will throw away his weapon and fall on his knees in front of his pursuers he may escape death, and in other dangers there are always ways of escaping death, if you are unscrupulous enough to say or do anything. The difficulty, my friends, is not in escaping death, but in escaping doing wrong, for that travels swifter than death. I am old and move slowly, and the slower one has overtaken me, but even though my accusers are quick and energetic, the faster runner, which is iniquity, has overtaken them.

When I leave this place, condemned by you to death, they too will go their ways, condemned by truth herself to suffer their own malevolence and heartlessness. As I must live with my sentence they too must live with theirs. I suppose these things may be regarded as fated – and I think that we must accept the outcome.

And now, to those of you who have condemned me, I feel moved to prophesy to you; for the hour of death is when we are gifted with prophetic power. I prophesy to you, my murderers, that immediately after my death a punishment far heavier than you have inflicted on me will surely fall upon you. You are executing me because you want to escape any criticism of your conduct, and not to have to give an account of your lives. But I prophesy that the result will not be as you suppose: in fact, quite the opposite. In future there will be many more judges for you than there are now for me; judges who up till now I have restrained – and as they are younger than me they will be even more severe on you, and you will be even more antagonised by them. If you think that by killing people you can avoid an examination of your wrong way of life, you are mistaken, for that is a way of escape that is neither possible nor honourable. The easiest and noblest way is not by crushing others, but by improving yourselves. This is the prophecy I utter before my departure, to those who have condemned me.

My friends, you who voted for my acquittal, I would also like to say a few words to you about this event, while the magistrates are busy, and before I go to the place of execution. Stay with me, so we can talk while there is still time. You are my friends, and I would like you to understand the correct way of understanding this event.

Gentlemen of the jury – for it is you who deserve to be truly called judges – I would like to tell you of a remarkable experience. Until now my inner oracle has constantly been in the habit of opposing me, even about trivial things, if I was about to make a mistake or error. Now as you can see, something has happened which may be thought, and is generally believed to be, the final and worst evil, but my oracle gave me no sign of opposition, either as I was leaving my house this morning, or when I was going into the court, or at any point in my speech. The oracle has often stopped me in the middle of a sentence, but this time it has not opposed anything I either said or did.

What's the explanation of this? I'll tell you. I regard this as proof that what has happened to me is in fact a blessing, and that we're mistaken in thinking that death is an evil. I have good grounds for saying this, for if the way I handled my case was not going to bring some good result the sign would surely have stopped me.

If we reflect on this in another way we shall see that there is much reason to hope that death is a blessing. Death is one of two things – either it's a state of utter annihilation and complete unconsciousness, or, as most people believe, it's a migration of the soul from this world to another. Now if you suppose that in death there is no consciousness, but only a deep sleep undisturbed even by dreams, that would be a priceless gain. If you were to select the night in which you slept so soundly as to not even dream, and were to compare this with all the other nights of your life, and then were told to say how many nights you had passed in your entire life more pleasantly than this one, I don't think that anyone, not even the great King of Persia, would find many such nights, when compared with the others. Now if death is like this, I say that to die is a blessing; for eternity can then be regarded as no more than a single night.

But if death is a journey to another place, and all the dead are there, as people think, what blessing, my friends and judges, can be greater than this? If, when the pilgrim arrives in the world below, he is freed from the so-called judges of this world, and finds the true judges who are said to reside there, Minos, Rhadamanthus, Aeacus and Triptolemus, and the other demi-gods who were righteous in their own lives, then that pilgrimage is worth making. What wouldn't you give to talk to Orpheus, Musaeus, Hesiod and Homer? If this is true, I am willing to die many times over. I would be thrilled to meet Palamedes, and Ajax, the son of Telamon, and all the other heroes of old who have suffered death through injustice. It would be amusing, I think, to compare my own calamity with theirs. Above all, I will be able to continue there my search into true and false knowledge, finding out who is really wise, and who is merely a pretender. What would one give, gentlemen, to be able to question the leader of the great Trojan expedition, or Odysseus, or Sisyphus, or countless other men and women! What unimaginable happiness there would be in speaking, mingling and arguing with them! I presume that in that world they do not put a man to death for just talking. For besides being happier in that world than here, they are immortal, if what we are told is true.

Therefore, my judges, take death lightly, and know this as a truth – that nothing can harm a good man, either in life or after death, and his fortunes are not neglected by the gods. My own approaching end has not happened by mere chance. I see clearly that to die and to be released from my mission was really better for me, and that is why my sign never turned me back. This is also why I am not angry with my accusers or my judges; they have not done me any real harm, although it wasn't with any kind intention that they did so, but because they thought they were harming me; and that is something for which I can gently blame them.

And now I have one favour to ask of you. When my sons are grown up, I would ask you, my friends, to trouble them, as I have troubled you, if they seem to care about riches, or anything else, more than about virtue. If they pretend to be something when they are really nothing, then reprove them, as I have reproved you, for not caring about that for which they ought to care, and thinking that they are something when they are really nothing. If you will do this for me, I and my sons will have had justice at your hands.

Now it is time for me to depart, and we must go our own ways – I to die, and you to live. Which is better God alone knows. Goodbye, my friends, and thank you for your kind support.

(Socrates is led away by the magistrates to the place of execution.)

2

SOCRATES IN PRISON

(Plato's Crito*)*
Should I Escape?

Socrates was meant to have been executed the day after sentencing, but because it was the time of the Delian religious festival, no executions could take place. So Socrates and his friends had thirty extra days in which they could meet in his prison cell. As usual, they talked about philosophy, virtue and wisdom, but there was one new topic on their minds: escape.

Plato recounts a time when the festival was nearing its end. When it finished and the ship from Delos arrived, the execution would take place. Crito, Socrates' childhood friend, and a wealthy farmer and landowner, comes to the prison to ask him if he would be willing to escape.

Scene: Socrates' prison. Pre-dawn

The door to Socrates' room opens slowly and Crito peers gently around the door. He is white-haired, around seventy years old, and is one of Socrates' oldest friends, having grown up with him. Seeing Socrates awake, he closes the door and walks in. He is carrying a basket.

Socrates is sitting on his bed and notices him.

SOCRATES: Crito, what are you doing here? It must be very early.

CRITO: It is, Socrates.

SOCRATES: How early?

Crito crosses over to a table and puts down his basket. He begins to take figs out of it and puts them in a bowl.

CRITO: Dawn is just breaking. I've brought you some figs.

SOCRATES: I'm surprised the guard let you in so early.

CRITO: I'm here so often, Socrates, he knows me by now; Anyway, I did him a little favour.

SOCRATES: Did you just arrive?

CRITO: No, I've been here a while.

SOCRATES: Crito, why did you wait, instead of waking me?

CRITO: Socrates, *I* can't sleep because I'm so miserable. But I was so amazed at how peacefully you were sleeping, and that was the reason I didn't wake you, because I wanted you to be out of pain. I've always thought you were happy because of your calm temperament; but I have never seen anyone bear such a calamity so easily and cheerfully.

SOCRATES: A man my age shouldn't be bitter at the prospect of death.

CRITO: Well, I've seen plenty of old men face similar problems, and age didn't stop them from whining.

SOCRATES: That may be. Anyway, you still haven't told me why you're here so early.

CRITO: Well, Socrates I came to bring you a message which is both sad and painful; perhaps not to you but certainly to all of us who are your friends, and saddest of all to me.

SOCRATES: What is it! I suppose the ship from Delos has arrived, and now the execution can go ahead.

CRITO: No, the ship hasn't actually arrived, but she'll probably get here today, since travellers from Sunium told me they saw the ship there; and so tomorrow, Socrates, will be the last day of your life.

SOCRATES: Very well, Crito; if that is the will of God, then I am willing; but I think there will be a day's delay.

CRITO: Why do you say that?

SOCRATES: I'll tell you. I am meant to die on the day after the arrival of the ship?

CRITO: That's what the authorities say.

SOCRATES: Well, I think the ship won't get here until tomorrow; I picked this up from a vision I had last night, or rather just now, when you fortunately allowed me to sleep.

CRITO: What kind of vision?

SOCRATES: It was a woman, lovely and graceful, dressed all in white, and she floated up and said: 'O Socrates – three days from now, to Phthia shall you go.'

CRITO: What an astonishing dream!

SOCRATES: No doubt about the meaning, Crito.

CRITO: Yes: the meaning is all too clear. My friend, let me beg you once more to take my advice and escape. Because, if you die, it's not just that I will lose a friend who can never be replaced, but there is another complication: people who don't know us will believe that I could have saved you if I had been willing to spend the money, but that I didn't care. Can there be a worse disgrace than this – that people would think Crito values money more than the life of his friend? People will refuse to believe that I wanted you to escape, but that you refused.

SOCRATES: Poor Crito, why care about their opinions? Good people, who are the only ones worth considering, will think about these things as they truly happened.

CRITO: But Socrates, can't you see that the opinion of the crowd has to be considered – look at your own case – since they can do the greatest evil to anyone they turn against?

SOCRATES: I only wish, Crito, that they could; because then they could also do the greatest good, and that would be excellent. But the truth is, they can't do either good or evil: they can't make a person wise or make them foolish; whatever they do is just the result of chance.

CRITO: Well, I won't dispute that. But tell me, Socrates, are you acting out of concern for me and your other friends:

are you afraid that if you escape we will get into trouble with the informers for having freed you, and lose our property, or that something even worse may happen to us? If this is what is worrying you, then stop; because to save you, we would surely run this or even greater risk; and escaping from here isn't very difficult.

SOCRATES: Crito, that is one of my fears, but it isn't the only one.

CRITO: At least drop that fear. We have friends who run no great risk and who are willing to save you from this prison; as for the informers, they are not being outrageous in their demands, and a little money will satisfy them. My means, which you know are ample, are at your service, and if you are concerned about spending only mine, there are others who will give you theirs; one of them, Simmias, has brought some money from Thebes for this purpose; and Cebes and many others are willing to help us too. So on that account do not hesitate about escaping, and please don't say, as you did in court, that you will have difficulty in knowing what to do with yourself if you escaped. For men will admire you no matter where you go, and not only in Attica; I have friends in Thessaly who will welcome and protect you, if you would like to go there, and no one will give you any trouble.

You are not justified, Socrates, in betraying your own life when you could be saved; this is playing into the hands of your enemies and destroyers; and frankly I think you are also betraying your children; for you could raise and educate them instead of going away and leaving them to take their chances; if they don't meet the usual fate of orphans, it won't be thanks to you. No one should bring children into the world unless they are willing to persevere to the end in their care and education. Frankly, I think you are choosing the easy way out, not the better and braver one, which really would have suited someone who professes virtue in all his actions, like yourself.

In fact, I am ashamed, not only of you, but of us, your

friends, when I reflect that this whole business of yours will be attributed to our lack of courage. This trial should never have taken place, or else it should have had another conclusion; and the end of it all, which is the height of absurdity, is that it will seem to have been allowed by us, through cowardice and apathy, who could have saved you, just as you could have saved yourself, if we had been good for anything; and we did not see how disgraceful and miserable, Socrates, all this would be to us as well as to you. You must make your mind up, or rather have it already decided; the time for deliberation is over, and there is only one thing to be done, which must be done, if at all, tonight, and any delay will make it all but impossible; I urge you therefore, Socrates, to let me convince you, and do as I say.

SOCRATES: Dear Crito, your zeal is admirable, if it is in the right; but if wrong, the greater the zeal the greater the harm; and so we need to consider whether we should do these things or not. For I am and always have been of a nature that must be guided by reason, whatever the reason that on reflection seems to me to be the best one; and now this event has happened, I can't discard the reasons that I previously gave: the principles that earlier I honoured and revere I still honour, and unless we are able to find other and better principles very quickly, I am certain I can't agree with you; no, not even if the power of the multitude instigated many more arrests, convictions and deaths, frightening us like children with demonic terrors.

But what is the fairest way to consider the question? Shall I return to your old argument about peoples' opinions, of which some can be valued, and others should not be valued?

CRITO: That's as good a starting point as any.

SOCRATES: Now were we right in believing this before I was convicted? Or has that argument which was once good now proved to be just talk for the sake of talking; in fact, only an amusement, and complete nonsense? That is what I would like to consider with your help, Crito: if, given my present circumstances, this argument appears to be in any way different or not; and so should be accepted by me or disallowed.

This argument, which is accepted by many who consider themselves to be authorities, was that the opinions of some people are to be regarded, and the opinions of other people not to be regarded. Now you, Crito, are an impartial person who is not going to die tomorrow – at least, there doesn't seem to be much likelihood of this, and you therefore are not liable to be deceived by the circumstances in which you find yourself.

Tell me, then, whether I am right in saying that some opinions, and the opinions of some people only, are to be valued, and other opinions, and the opinions of other people, are not to be valued. I ask you whether I was right in accepting this?

CRITO: You were right.

SOCRATES: The opinions of good people are to be regarded, and not the opinions of the bad?

CRITO: Yes.

SOCRATES: And the opinions of the wise are good, and the opinions of the unwise are evil?

CRITO: Certainly.

SOCRATES: And what we said about the other subject? Was the gymnastics student supposed to listen to the praise, blame and opinions of everyone, or of one man only – his trainer, whoever that was?

CRITO: Of one man only.

SOCRATES: And should this gymnast fear the criticism and welcome the praise of that one person only, and not of the many?

CRITO: That is clear.

SOCRATES: And should he live and train, eat and drink in the way that seems good to this single instructor who has understanding, rather than according to the opinion of everyone else put together?

CRITO: He should.

SOCRATES: And if he disobeys and disregards the opinion and approval of the one, and regards the opinion of the many who have no understanding, will he not suffer harm?

CRITO: Certainly he will.

SOCRATES: And what will the harm be, what will it tend to affect, in the disobedient person?

CRITO: Clearly, it will affect his body; that is what will be harmed.

SOCRATES: Very good; and isn't this also true, Crito, of many other things? In questions concerning justice and injustice, fairness and partiality, good and evil, which are the subjects of our present discussion, should we follow the opinion of the many and fear them; or the opinion of the one person who has understanding, who we ought to fear and respect more than all the rest of the world: and if we desert that person we shall injure and destroy that principle in us which we can assume will be improved by justice and degraded by injustice; isn't there such a principle?

CRITO: Certainly there is, Socrates.

SOCRATES: Take a parallel case; if, acting under the advice of men who have no understanding, we destroy what can be improved by health and degraded by disease – and here I mean the body – when that has been destroyed, would life be worth having?

CRITO: No.

SOCRATES: Could we live, having an evil and corrupted body?

CRITO: Certainly not.

SOCRATES: And will life be worth having, if the higher part of man, the part that is improved by justice and degraded by injustice, becomes corrupted? Do we consider this principle, whatever it may be in man, that has to do with justice and injustice, to be inferior to the body?

CRITO: Certainly not.

SOCRATES: In fact more honoured?

CRITO: Much more honoured.

SOCRATES: Then, my friend, we must not regard what the many say of us: but only regard what he, the one person who has understanding of just and unjust, will say, and what the truth will say. And therefore, you begin in error when you suggest that we should listen to the opinion of the many about just and unjust, good and evil, honourable and dishonourable. Now someone will probably say, 'But the many can kill us.'

CRITO: Yes, Socrates; that will clearly be the answer.

SOCRATES: That is true; but I'm still surprised to find that the old argument is, I think, as solid as ever. And I would like to know whether I can say the same of another proposition – that it is not just life that we should value, but a good life above all?

CRITO: Yes, that also remains true.

SOCRATES: And a good life is equivalent to a just and honourable one – that holds also?

CRITO: Yes, that holds.

SOCRATES: Now, from these premises I can proceed to argue the question of whether I should or should not try to escape without the consent of the Athenians: and if I am clearly right in escaping, then I will make the attempt; but if not, I must decline.

The other considerations you mention, of money and loss of character, and the duty of educating children, are, I am afraid, only the doctrines of the multitude, who would be as ready to bring people to life, if they were able, as they are to put them to death – and with as little reason.

But now, since the argument has so far prevailed, the only question that remains to be considered is, whether we shall be correct either by escaping or by letting others aid our escape and paying them in money and thanks, or whether we shall not be correct; and if it is the latter, then death or any other calamity that may ensue on my remaining here must not be allowed to enter into the calculation.

CRITO: Unfortunately you are right, Socrates; how shall we proceed?

SOCRATES: Let us discuss it together, and if you are able to refute me I will be convinced; if not, then cease, dear friend, from repeating to me that I ought to escape against the wishes of the Athenians: for I really would like to be persuaded by you, but not against my own better judgement.

Now, please consider my first position, and do your best to answer me.

CRITO: I will do my best.

SOCRATES: Can we say that we should never intentionally do wrong, or that sometimes we should and at other times we should not do wrong, or is doing wrong always evil and dishonourable, as we have already acknowledged? Are all the things we agreed during the last few days to be thrown away?

And have we, at our age, been earnestly discussing with one another all of our life, only to discover that we are no better than children?

Or are we to remain assured, in spite of the opinion of the many, and in spite of the consequences whether better or worse, of the truth of what we said, that injustice is always an evil and dishonour to the person who acts unjustly? Can we affirm that?

CRITO: Yes.

SOCRATES: Then we must not do wrong?

CRITO: Certainly not.

SOCRATES: Not even if injured to commit an injury in return, which is how most people think; we must never injure anyone at all?

CRITO: Clearly not.

SOCRATES: Again, Crito, should we do evil?

CRITO: Surely not, Socrates.

SOCRATES: And what about doing evil in return for evil, which is the morality of the many – is that just or not?

CRITO: Not just.

SOCRATES: Because doing evil to another person is the same as injuring him?

CRITO: Very true.

SOCRATES: Then we should not retaliate or exchange evil for evil to anyone, whatever evil we may have suffered from them. But I want you to consider, Crito, whether you really mean what you are saying. For this opinion has never been held, and never will be held, by a large number of people; and those who agree and disagree about this point have no common ground, and can only despise one another, when they see how widely they differ. Tell me, then, whether you agree with and assent to my first principle, that neither injury nor retaliation nor warding off evil by evil is ever right.

Will that be the premise of our agreement, or do you decline and disagree with this? For this has always been, and is still, my opinion; but, if you have another opinion, let me hear it. If, however, you remain of the same mind as before, I will proceed to the next step.

CRITO: Proceed, for I have not changed my mind.

SOCRATES: Good. Then the next step can be put as a question: should a person do what he considers to be right, or should he betray that right?

CRITO: He should do what he thinks right.

SOCRATES: If this is true, how do we apply it? If I leave prison against the will of the Athenians, do I harm anyone? Or do I, in reality, harm those whom I should harm the least? Don't I desert the principles which we acknowledged to be just? What do you say?

CRITO: I don't really know, Socrates. I can't say.

SOCRATES: Then look at it in this way: imagine that I am about to play truant (you can call the event by any name you like), and the laws and the government come to interrogate me.

'Tell us, Socrates,' they say, 'what are you doing? Are you trying to overturn us, the state and its laws, by this act of yours, as far as you are able? Do you believe that a state in which the decisions of law have no power, but can be pushed aside and overthrown by individuals, can subsist and not be overthrown?'

What will we answer, Crito, to this and similar words? Anyone, and especially a clever rhetorician, will have a great deal to say about the evil of pushing aside a law which requires a sentence to be carried out. So we might reply, 'Yes; but the state has injured us and given an unjust sentence.' Suppose I were to say that?

CRITO: That's fair, Socrates.

SOCRATES: Then the law would say to me, 'Was that our agreement with you, or were you to live with the sentence of the state?' And if I were to express astonishment at their saying this, the law would probably add: 'Answer us, Socrates, instead of looking so wide-eyed: you are in the habit of asking and answering questions. Tell us what your complaint is against us that justifies your attempt to destroy us and the state? In the first place, didn't we bring you into existence? Your father married your mother with our aid and conceived you. Tell us if you have any objection to make against those of us who regulate marriage?' None, I would reply.

'Or against those of us who regulate the system of nurture and education of children in which you were trained? Weren't the laws, which are in charge of this, right in ordering your father to train you in music and gymnastics?' Right, I would reply. 'Well, then, since you were brought into the world, nurtured and educated by us, can you deny in the first place that you are our child and servant, as your fathers were before you? And if this is true you are not on equal terms with us; nor can you think that you have a right to do to us what we are doing to you. Do you have the right to strike or revile or do any other evil to your father or to your master, if you had one, when you have been struck or reviled by him, or received some other harm by him? – you would not say you do? And because we think it right to destroy you, do you think that you have any right to destroy us in return, and your country as far as you are able?

'And will you, O professor of true virtue, say that you are justified in this? Has a philosopher like you failed to discover that our country is far higher and holier than any mother, father or ancestor, and is to be more valued and regarded in the eyes of the gods and of people of under-standing? And it is to be comforted, and gently and rever-ently appealed to when angry, even more than a father, and even if not persuaded by her, obeyed? And when we are punished by her, whether with imprisonment or the whip, that punishment is to be suffered in silence; and if she leads us to wounds or death in battle, there we follow as is right; and no one can either yield or retreat or leave his rank, but whether in battle or in a court of law, or in any other place, he must do what his city and his country order him; or he must change their view of what is just: and if he can not be violent to his father or mother, so much less can he be violent to his country.'

What answer can we give to this, Crito? Do the laws speak truly, or not?

CRITO: I think they do.

SOCRATES: Then the laws will say: 'Consider, Socrates, if this is true, that in your present attempt you are going to do us wrong. For, after having brought you into the world, and nurtured and educated you, and given you and every other citizen a share in every good that we had to give, we further proclaim and give the right to every Athenian, that if he does not like us when he has come of age and has seen the ways of the city, and made our acquaintance, he may go where he pleases and take his goods with him; and none of us laws will stop him or interfere with him.

'Any of you who does not like us and the city, and who wants to go to a colony or to any other city, may go where he likes, and take his goods with him. But the person who has experience of the way in which we administer justice and the State, and still remains, has entered into an implied contract that he will do as we command him.

'And the person who disobeys us is, as we maintain, wrong three times over: first, because in disobeying us he is disobeying his parents; secondly, because we are the authors of his education; thirdly, because he has made an agreement with us that he will duly obey our commands; and if he fails to obey them and does not convince us that they are wrong, and we do not harshly impose them, but give him the alternative of obeying them or convincing us; that is what we offer but he does neither. These are the kinds of accusations which you, Socrates, will be exposed to if you play truant; you, above all other Athenians.'

Suppose I were to ask, why is that? They will justly reply that I above all other men have acknowledged this agreement. 'There is clear proof,' they will say, 'Socrates, that we and the city were not displeasing to you. Of all Athenians you have been the most permanent of all residents, which, since you never want to leave, you must be supposed to love. For you never leave the city either to see the games, except once, or to any other place unless when you were on military service. You did not travel as other men do, and had no curiosity to know other states or their laws: your affections did not go beyond us and our state; we were your especial favourites, and you acquiesced in our government of you; and this is the state in which you conceived your children, which is a proof of your satisfaction. In any case, during your trial you could, if you had liked, have set the punishment at banishment – the state which now refuses to let you go would have let you go then. But you pretended that you preferred death to exile, and that you were not dejected about death. And now you have forgotten those fine sentiments, and pay no respect to us, the laws, of whom you are the destroyer; and are doing what only a miserable slave would do, running away and turning your back upon the contracts and agreements which you made as a citizen.

'But first of all answer this question: are we right in saying that you agreed to be governed by us in deed, and not just in word only? Is that true or not?'

How shall we answer that, Crito? Must we not agree?

CRITO: There is no help for it, Socrates.

SOCRATES: Then will they not say: 'You, Socrates, are breaking the contracts and agreements which you made with us at your leisure, not in haste or under compulsion or deception, but having had seventy years to think of them, during which time you were free to leave the city, if we were not to your liking, or if our covenants appeared to you to be unfair. You had your choice, and could have gone to either Sparta or Crete, which you often praise for their good government, or to any other Hellenic or foreign state. Whereas you, above all other Athenians, seemed to be so fond of the state, or, in other words, of us her laws (for who would want a state that had no laws?), that you never left her: the disabled, the blind, the maimed, were not more stationary in her than you were.

'And now you run away and abandon your agreements. Don't do it, Socrates, take our advice; don't make yourself ridiculous by escaping from the city. What good will you do, either for yourself or for your friends, if you transgress in this sort of way? It is pretty certain that your friends will be driven into exile and deprived of citizenship, or lose their property; and you, Socrates, if you run to one of our neighbouring cities, such as Thebes or Megara, both of which are well-governed places, you will arrive there as an enemy, and their governments will be against you, and all patriotic citizens will cast an evil eye on you as a destroyer of the laws, and you will confirm in the minds of our judges the correctness of their verdict of you.

'For someone who is a corrupter of the laws is more than likely to be a corrupter of the young and foolish. Perhaps you should avoid well-run cities and virtuous people? Is life worth having on these terms? Or will you go to them without shame, and talk to them, Socrates? And what will you discourse about? What you say here about virtue, justice, institutions and laws being humanity's greatest gifts? Would that be decent of you? Surely not. But if you go away from well-governed states to Crito's friends in Thessaly, where there is great disorder and license, they will be charmed to hear the tale of your escape from prison, embellished with ludicrous details of the way that you were wrapped in a goatskin or some other disguise, and metamorphosed into the fashion of a runaway – that is very likely; and will there be no one to remind you that in your old age you violated the most sacred laws from a miserable desire for a scrap more of life? Maybe not, if you keep them in a good mood; but if they get upset you will hear many degrading things; yes, you will live, but how – as everyone's flatterer and everyone's servant; and to do what? – eating and drinking in Thessaly, having gone abroad so that you can get fed. And where will all your fine sentiments about justice and virtue be then? Or if you say that you desire to live for the sake of your children, so you can raise and educate them – will you take them to Thessaly and deprive them of Athenian citizenship? Is that the benefit you want to give them? Or are you under the impression that they will be better cared for and educated here if you are still alive, although not actually present, since your friends will take care of them? Do you imagine that if you were living in Thessaly they would take care of them, and if you were an inhabitant of the other world they would not take care of them? No; but if they who call themselves friends are truly friends, they surely will.

'Listen to us, Socrates, who have raised you. Don't think of life and children first, and of justice second, but of justice first, so that you can be justified before the rulers of the world below. For neither will you nor any of your family be happier, holier or more just in this life, or happier in another, if you do as Crito suggests. Now you must depart in innocence, a sufferer of evil and not a doer of it; a victim, not of the laws, but of people. But if you move off, returning evil for evil, and injury for injury, breaking the contracts and agreements that you made with us, and doing wrong to those whom you should least wrong, that is to say, yourself, your friends, your country, and us, we shall be angry with you while you live, and our brothers, the laws in the world below, will receive you there as an enemy; for they will know that you have done your best to destroy us. Listen Socrates, to us, and not to Crito.'

This is the voice that I seem to hear murmuring in my ears, like the sound of a flute in the ears of a mystic; this voice is humming in my ears, and stops me from hearing any other. And I know that anything more that you say will be in vain.

But do speak, if there is anything more to add.

CRITO: I have nothing more to say, Socrates.

SOCRATES: Then Crito, my good friend, let me follow the whisperings of the will of God.

3

NOW THE HOUR OF SUNSET WAS NEAR

(From Plato's Phaedo*)*

*S*ocrates' friends, his wife Xanthippe and his children visited
him on his last day, and when his wife started weeping
he asked his friends to take her and the children away. But
his friends stayed with him to the very end.

Now the hour of sunset was near . . . the prison officer walked
into the room and said to him, 'Socrates, since you are the
noblest, gentlest and best of all the men who ever came here,
I am sure you will not get angry with me like the others, who
raged and swore at me when, in obedience to the magistrates,
I told them to drink the poison. I am sure you will not be
angry with me because it is others, and not I, who are responsible for this. You know what I must do now, so try to bear
lightly what you must endure. Then, saying goodbye, he burst
into tears, turned away and went out.

Socrates looked at his departing figure and said, 'I return
your good wishes, and will do as you bid.' Then, turning to
us, he said, 'How charming the man is: since I have been in
prison he has been coming to see me, and at times he would
talk to me, and was as good as could be to me, and now see
how generously he grieves for me. But we must do as he says,

Crito; let the cup be brought, if the poison is prepared: if not, let the attendant prepare some.'

'But,' said Crito, 'the sun is still above the hilltops, and many have taken the poison late, and, even after the announcement was made, have eaten and drunk and enjoyed themselves; there is still time, do not hurry.'

Socrates said: 'Crito, they may have been right in doing this, for they thought that they would gain by the delay; but I am right in not doing it this way, for I do not think that I shall gain anything by drinking the poison a little later; I would just be sparing and saving a life which is already gone, and I could only laugh at myself for this. Please do as I say, and don't refuse me.'

Crito, when he heard this, made a sign to the servant, and the servant went in, and remained for some time, and then returned with the jailer carrying a cup of poison. Socrates said: 'You, my good friend, who are experienced in these matters, give me directions as to how I am to proceed.' The man answered, 'You have only to walk around until your legs get heavy, and then lie down, and the poison will act.' He handed the cup to Socrates, who in the easiest and gentlest manner, without the least fear or change of colour or feature, looking directly at the man as his manner was, took the cup and said, 'What do you say about making a libation out of this cup to a god? May I, or not?' The man answered, 'We only prepare, Socrates, just as much as we think will be enough.'

'I understand,' he said. 'Yet I may and must pray to the gods to prosper my journey from this to that other world. May this, which is my prayer, be granted to me.'

Then, holding the cup to his lips, quite readily and cheerfully he drank the poison. Up to now most of us had been able to control our sorrow; but now when we saw him drinking, and saw too that he had drained the cup, we could no longer contain ourselves, and in spite of myself my own tears were flowing fast. I covered my face and wept over myself, for certainly I was not weeping over him, but at the thought of my own calamity in having lost such a companion. Nor was I the first, for Crito, when he found himself unable to restrain his tears, had got up and moved away, and I followed; and at that moment. Apollodorus, who had been weeping all the time, broke out in a loud cry which made cowards of us all. Socrates alone retained his calmness,

'What is this strange outcry? I sent the women away so they might not offend in this way, for I have heard that a man should die in peace. Be quiet, then, and have patience.'

When we heard that, we were ashamed, and held back our tears, and he walked some more until, as he said, his legs began to fail, and then he lay on his back, and the man who gave him the poison now and then looked at his feet and legs; and after a while he pressed his foot hard and asked him if he could feel; and Socrates said, no; and then his leg, and so upwards and upwards, and showed us that he was cold and stiff. And he felt them himself, and said, 'When the poison reaches the heart, that will be the end.'

He was beginning to grow cold around his groin, when he uncovered his face, for he had covered himself up, and said (and they were his last words) – he said:

'Crito, I owe a cock to Asclepius. Will you remember to pay the debt?'

'The debt shall be paid,' said Crito. 'Is there anything else?'

There was no answer to this question; but in a minute or two a movement was heard, and the attendants uncovered him. His eyes were set, and Crito closed his eyes and mouth.

Such was the end of our friend, whom I may truly call the wisest, and justest, and best of all the men whom I have ever known.